"Wendy Blight has long been a trusted voice and *Rest for Your Soul* delivers everything the title promises. Wendy combines practical steps and scriptural insight with her trademark gentleness, drawing us into connection with Christ via life-changing 'holy habits.' This book is a powerful companion to your prayer life. It will leave you refreshed, renewed, and—yes—genuinely rested, even in life's busiest and most unsettling seasons."

—**JODIE BERNDT,** bestselling author of
Praying the Scriptures for Your Life

"We live in an increasingly restless world, where panic and anxiety seem to be around every corner. I've often thought, 'Is rest in this life even a reality?' Thankfully, my friend and Bible teacher Wendy Blight shows us convincingly and winsomely that rest is indeed possible for our souls. At every turn of the page, Wendy reminds us that our hearts are restless because we often allow distance to intrude between us and the God who created us to find our rest in Him. This is a deeply biblical, theological, and applicable book that will encourage you today and equip you for tomorrow."

—**DR. JOEL MUDDAMALLE,** director of theology
and research, Proverbs 31 Ministries

"I have walked through many seasons where, as Wendy would say, my 'emotions have taken my soul hostage,' but I didn't have the language to help me understand or navigate what was happening. Wendy's powerful book, *Rest for Your Soul*, fills in what I was lacking. When studying how to create space for the holy habits of solitude, silence, and prayer, you want to trust that the author has lived this type of life out. I can assure you that Wendy has done this, and you will benefit immensely from her wisdom and the tools she offers for practical application of these practices. Read this book with great anticipation of how the Holy Spirit will do His supernatural 'soul-settling' work *in* you as Wendy guides you into God's truth!"

—**JEANNIE CUNNION,** bestselling author of *Don't Miss Out*

"If you're weary of being stuck in a cycle of fear, anxious thoughts, and deep overwhelm which you can't seem to get a handle on, *Rest for Your Soul* couldn't come at a better time. My trusted friend Wendy will guide and help you implement habits into your days which could transform your life. Let the practices of silence, solitude, and prayer draw you closer to God as His peace settles all around you. Don't miss this amazing resource!"

—LYSA TERKEURST, #1 *New York Times* bestselling
author and president of Proverbs 31 Ministries

"I love anything and everything Wendy Blight writes. She is the real thing, having a voice of empathy and wisdom. Wendy gets right to my heart with her sound biblical insight and practical applications, because she lives out what she teaches. So, if you deal with all the things that come with being human . . . like anxiety, uncertainty, or weariness, let Wendy walk you back to rest."

—JENNIFER ROTHSCHILD, bestselling author,
4:13 Podcast host, Bible study teacher, and founder
of Fresh Grounded Faith Women's Events

REST FOR YOUR SOUL

A Bible Study on
Solitude, Silence, and Prayer

WENDY BLIGHT

Harper*Christian*
Resources

Rest for Your Soul
© 2023 by Wendy Blight

Requests for information should be addressed to:
HarperChristian Resources, 3900 Sparks Dr. SE, Grand Rapids, Michigan 49546

ISBN 978-0-310-15947-6 (softcover)
ISBN 978-0-310-15948-3 (ebook)

Author represented by Wolgemuth and Associates.

First Printing May 2023

CONTENTS

TIPS FOR OUR JOURNEY TOGETHER

All through the writing of this study, I thought about *you*. I not only thought about you; I prayed for you. I prayed for every person who would one day hold this book in her hand.

How I wish we were sitting across from each other at my kitchen table so I could hear your heart and know your story! We'd have our Bibles open, enjoying some of my friend Nancy's delicious homemade granola (see the appendix section for the recipe).

Please don't think of this as a traditional Bible study, though you will find Bible verses and teachings tucked into its pages. Rather, think of this as an invitation to join me on a journey that will create more space in your life for God through what I call the holy habits of solitude, silence, and prayer. It is a journey where you will drink deeply from God's sacred well of living water and allow that living water to do supernatural soul-settling work. Along the way, I'll share bits and pieces of my story and the stories of some dear friends.

We'll spend most of our time together engaging our hearts and minds with one book. That book is the Bible—God's Word. It's a book unlike any other in history because of its Author. The Bible has an all-loving, all-powerful, all-knowing force behind the words on each page. And that force, the One who sent the words, is the One who created, shaped, and molded you. He then filled you with His Spirit so you could access His wisdom, knowledge, understanding, and power.

As you gather your materials, you'll need a Bible for sure. If you have a favorite translation, use that. I'll be mostly using the NIV. You'll find questions scattered throughout each chapter, so I encourage you to have a journal or notebook to help you better engage with God, His Word, and your heart as you work through the questions. I promise you that those words you write will be a gift, especially on those hard days when you find your unsettledness pressing its way back in, stealing your peace. You will need reminders of the truths you've memorized, the promises you've prayed, and the challenges you've overcome to fight back.

Also, please know that I'm not writing this because I now live every day with a settled soul. I don't. But I do recognize when those unsettled emotions sneak up on me, and I know I have the truths and tools I need to interrupt and redirect them. I know the sacred pauses to take, the truths to declare, and the prayers to pray to refresh and restore my soul.

More than anything as we begin, I want you to know you're not alone. We're doing this together. Every. Step. Of. The. Way.

Let's pray:

Father God, we invite You into our time together. We trust as we meet You in our moments of solitude, silence, and prayer that You will tenderly minister to the anxious spaces and shattered places of our hearts. We choose today to believe that You will use each leg of our journey to bring us closer to healing, strength, and victory. In Jesus's name, amen.

Introduction

LORD, WHAT'S WRONG WITH ME?

MESSAGE FROM MY HEART

Lord, please settle my unsettled soul. This was the daily, sometimes hourly, cry of my heart several years ago. An unceasing, all-consuming unsettledness I didn't want to feel, deal with, or even speak of because if I didn't, maybe it would go away. But it didn't.

I remember walking through stores or being with friends and wondering, *Why can't I feel normal like they do? What's happening inside me? Why can't I shake this intense uneasiness?*

Even more frustratingly, I had no idea why I was experiencing this. It felt so unfair! I wanted it to stop. I pleaded and begged for God to take it away. But month after month I heard nothing. *God, are You really with me? Do You see me? Care about me? Love me? Where are You?*

There were so many long, difficult, tear-filled middle-of-the-nights. It was one of the hardest, loneliest times in my life. With each day I turned more and more inward, sheltering in place, avoiding anything and anyone that required time and energy from me. I knew things had to change, but I wasn't sure of the steps I needed to take to get there. I was angry with God, but at the same time, deep in my heart, I knew He was the answer.

This is the story I'm here to share with you. And statistics reveal I'm not alone. A 2018 study by the American Psychiatric Association revealed that 51 percent of Americans describe themselves as anxious, tipping the scales in favor of worry for the first time.[1]

Have your emotions taken your life hostage? Do you have an unsettled soul? Do you live in a continued state of anxiety or fear? Are you exhausted from fighting this battle? So was I, friend. And some days, I still am. Life's circumstances, problems, and relationships can lead our souls into the deepest unsettledness, despair, and grief. Yet I came to realize that turning inward only exacerbated my emotions. I knew if I wanted to see God, feel God, and experience God in this place, I needed to shift my perspective. I needed to stop turning inward and turn my eyes upward—take my eyes off myself and fix them on Him.

God took me on a journey that invited me to dive deeply into what the church calls "spiritual disciplines"—solitude, silence, and prayer. But these didn't feel like disciplines to me. Rather, they became desperately needed sacred pauses in my day. These pauses allowed my weary, thirsty soul to drink deeply from God's always accessible well of living water. These holy habits over time redirected my emotions, renewed my mind, and refreshed my soul.

These days I look back and know deep down inside that what I really needed was the confidence that God was with me. That He saw me, heard me, and loved me.

At one point along the way, I heard God's still small voice: *You're not alone. Trust me. I am with you.* God then impressed another thought on my heart: *As you turn upward, I also want you to look outward because you are not alone in this unsettled place.*

I took a step of faith, looked outward, invited a few friends in, and shared what God had been teaching me about the holy habits of solitude, silence, and prayer. God was right—I wasn't alone. The women I shared my story with also wrestled with their emotions. Some struggled with anxiety. Others grappled with fear, rejection, loneliness, or depression.

My personal journey, and the one I traveled alongside these women, inspired me to write the chapters and pages you'll be reading. As you read, begin by knowing that I'm not an expert. I'm just a woman who heard God's still small voice and took baby steps to obey. I'm a woman who discovered I wasn't alone in my unsettledness when I turned upward and outward. I wasn't alone in my wrestling. I wasn't alone in thinking I landed where I was because somewhere along the way I had failed God and myself. I wasn't alone in believing I wasn't strong enough or committed enough to do the hard work to get to the other side. I wasn't alone in believing I wasn't faithful enough to trust that God would be with me every step of the way.

I also want you to know as you read these words that each time I sat down to write, I prayed for God to bring His daughters who need Him to settle their souls so He can take them on the healing journey of solitude, silence, and prayer.

If you're reading these words and saying "that's me," this is your divine appointment—not with me, but with your Father in heaven. Please know that God hears the cry of your heart. He not only knows the tears you've cried, but Scripture tells us He's also collecting them (more about that later). And what about those long, sleepless nights when you lie awake wondering, *Will this ever end?* Please know that God is watching over you, even though He may feel a million miles away.

In fact, He's waiting for you. This is your invitation to take sacred pauses at His well. It is your invitation into the holy habits of solitude, silence, and prayer. Why do I call them holy "habits"? Because habits are small, intentional decisions we make over and over again without thinking. Author and speaker Justin Whitmel Earley says it well: "The tiny and subconscious nature of habits makes them powerful. Why? Because they create our 'normal.' Normal life is what stays with you from January through December. Normal life is what shapes your kids, your body, your schedule, and your heart."[2]

This is exactly what we're working toward in this book—to make sacred pauses with God our "norm." It is what we do, not just when we need God or when we feel bad because we haven't been with Him in a while. It's what we faithfully commit to do from January to December in whatever way works best with our schedule.

🌀 **What is your soul thirsting for?**

_____

_____

_____

🌀 **Often we look to other "wells" to fill our thirsty souls. What wells are you drinking from to fulfill your soul's thirsty places?**

_____

_____

_____

If you want to quench your thirsty soul and experience God's deep, abiding rest, walking in the assurance that He sees you, hears you, and loves you, accept this invitation so together we can drink deeply from God's sacred well and allow that living water to settle our unsettled souls.

Take baby steps into these holy habits with me. They are habits that will equip you to productively and effectively process your emotions and find the peace and settledness you're longing for.

Earlier I told you that I'll share bits and pieces of my story. As I do, I encourage you to keep your story in mind. Consider what you're feeling and experiencing as you read my words, along with God's Word.

MY STORY

A few years ago, anxiety hijacked my life in ways I could never have imagined. The very thought of leaving my house brought on severe panic attacks. Engaging with people in any manner or form overwhelmed me.

I struggled with even the smallest of tasks. I cried more than I didn't. I lay awake night after night after night.

The voice of shame reared its ugly head, taunting me. *You're a Christian. You shouldn't struggle with this. You should trust God. Your Bible tells you He's enough.* Yes, that's true. That's what I've been taught, and that's what I believed. But it wasn't what I was living. Instead, my faith was failing me. Or was it me failing my faith?

Next came guilt, because my calling is to teach God's Word. I'd been doing this for over a decade. I'd written a book on how to overcome fear, along with two Bible studies, and was nearing publication of my third study. I'm the woman people came to when they wanted help, and now I couldn't even help myself. I felt like an imposter.

After months with no change, I went to my internist with my symptoms. Battling a racing heart rate, generalized body aches and pains, digestive issues, constant sadness, and sleepless nights, I was hoping with all my heart that she would diagnose me with something she easily could fix. Instead, she told me I was suffering from severe anxiety and needed to make an appointment with a counselor.

So I did. I'd never done counseling before, and was thankful our church had a counseling department. I took the brave step and made an appointment.

My counselor, Rebecca, listened quietly as I shared my story. She prayed and invited God into our time together, then spoke honestly about where I was. The hardest part of that first session was how she shot down every expectation I had carried in. I wanted a quick fix and honestly expected that after a few visits I'd get some good tips and tools, my anxiety would go away, and my life would return to normal.

Instead, Rebecca informed me there was no easy fix—this would take time and hard work. She also warned me that my life might never go back to "normal," but promised me that if I invested in the hard, heart work, I would land in a healthier place—a better place. She clarified: *different but better.*

☙ **Remember, we're walking this together. I've shared my story. Will you share your story here? Take a few minutes. Record what you're feeling. Where are you on your journey? Tell God what's on your heart. Be honest—He can take it.**

_____

_____

_____

_____

_____

_____

Just a few visits into my counseling, Rebecca uncovered a series of events in my life that she called "the perfect storm."

Weather-wise, a perfect storm is a particularly violent storm arising from a rare combination of adverse and often unexpected factors in the atmosphere.

In life, a perfect storm is a rare combination of hard, often unpredictable events or circumstances that rush in all at once and produce an unusually bad or difficult result.

Rebecca explained that the winds and waves of a perfect storm had blown into my life. I told her that I'd battled hard seasons and emotions before, but I'd never fallen apart like this. What made this different? She explained that it wasn't just one or two events; many trials and losses had crashed through in a short amount of time.

My youngest, Bo, had left for college, leaving us a very quiet empty nest. Then at age fifty-two, my husband lost his job for the first time in his career.

One of my best friends tragically lost her twenty-year-old firefighter son while he was on duty. Our family had loved him like a son.

Probably the most devastating event of all, and the one that likely pushed me over the edge, was when a significant person walked out of my life, indicating that she no longer wanted to be part of it. I wish I could share more, but I can't. It's complicated and hard.

In the midst of it all, life went on. I was teaching a large women's Bible study in Charlotte, North Carolina, volunteering and writing for Proverbs 31 Ministries, and going through the final edits for my next book, which was to be released that year.

So much heartache. So much loss. So much responsibility.

Rebecca encouraged me by saying that I could have handled one or even a few of these waves of grief, hurt, and loss. But they had all rushed in at once. Wave after wave after wave.

Maybe you're there.

🕉 **What are the hard winds and waves in your storm? Where have they left you?**

Walking with God feels easy when things are going well. But it doesn't come so easily when life turns upside down.

God *felt* far away. He didn't *feel* present. It *seemed* like He didn't hear my prayers or see my tears. I *felt* forgotten.

I'm thankful for Rebecca. Her counseling ignited the tiny ember of faith that still burned in my heart. I hadn't felt it, nor was I aware of it. But that small, flaming ember took me on a step-by-step journey that gave me the faith, courage, and strength to press *through* that hard season.

Did you notice the word I emphasized—"through"? This reminded me of Rebecca's words that this journey to healing would be long and hard. It would take time.

"Through" tells us that we aren't going over or around our perfect storm. We aren't turning back to take another path to escape the storm. But we also aren't giving up in the middle of the storm.

No! We're pressing *through* the storm, step by step together. And though my story is anxiety, yours may be fear, grief, rejection, doubt, or unforgiveness. It's not the specific emotion that holds us hostage that matters on this journey. It's where that emotion leaves us personally and with God.

⟲ **What emotion is holding you hostage, causing you to turn inward?**

_____

_____

_____

Before my first visit with Rebecca, I wanted to give up. All I wanted was to be normal again. However, my first visit didn't alleviate those feelings. It was a hard session, because I knew by the end of our time together that this was not going away.

All my tools and my normal way of handling life weren't working anymore. I kept trying on my own and trying hard, but it wasn't enough. No matter how hard I tried and prayed, anxiety won. Every. Single. Time.

Initially, Rebecca's words brought on more panic attacks that left me paralyzed and feeling like I'd lost total control of my life. Which, of course, I had. I was living in survival mode.

Instead of dealing with my emotions, I coped and numbed them by binge-watching Netflix, old movies, and TV shows. That way, I didn't have to think about how out of control my life was.

But Rebecca spoke hard words—words that scared me. She said I had to spend time in quiet places where I could open up unattended to chapters and stories in my life and deal with them, one by one.

Nothing else had worked, so I made the decision to follow her wisdom and stop fighting my anxiety. I started a new routine. Every night, without fail, I went up to my room with my Bible and a journal. I had no agenda. This was the last thing I wanted to do because I harbored so much anger against God. I felt like He had forgotten me and was ignoring the cries of my heart. Honestly, I didn't want to show up—but I went out of obedience because I hadn't seen or heard God work in months and didn't feel much hope when I began.

Are you there right now? Do you awake in the night feeling

overwhelmed by what's happening in your life or in the world around you? Do you feel the heavy weight of heartbreak? Do you feel utterly alone, wondering whether God hears you? Whether He sees you? Maybe you're even asking yourself if He cares at all?

Friend, I understand! It's why I'm here with you, taking this journey. I want you to hear "me too!" or "I know!" I felt alone. Helpless and hopeless. Frustrated. Afraid I would never get to the other side.

But I did get there. It took time. It took commitment. It took discipline. Our out-of-control emotions don't tuck in their tails and walk away. They fight back. They wrestle and continue, even on the other side, to rear their ugly heads. They're relentless. That is why the biblical truths, holy habits, scientific research, and practical tools I share are for life, not just for this journey. They will equip you to battle and overcome whatever the Enemy brings into your life, whenever he brings it.

Let's pray together as we embark on our journey:

Heavenly Father, as we begin this journey, we begin with great expectation for all that You will do in our midst. God, we know how often we fail to give You first priority. We allow the busyness of life to push You aside. Yet we also long for peace and rest. We long to be in Your presence and hear Your voice, but we can't do so amidst our worries and fears. As we open our Bibles to study Your Word, reveal the places in our hearts that keep us from hearing You speak. Tender our hearts to uncover the root of our unsettledness and the cause of our unrest. Show us the places where we're imprisoned by our emotions or entangled in the things of this world. Free us from what holds us captive so we can grow deeper in our relationship with You. Show us how to slow down, to take sacred pauses, and to stop and drink at Your sacred well. Redirect our emotions. Restore and renew our minds. Refresh our souls. Help us to truly know how wide and high and deep and long is Your love and to walk fully in that love. We love You, Lord, and thank You in advance for all You will do in our lives as we begin this journey into the holy habits of solitude, silence, and prayer. We ask this in Jesus's name, amen.

LORD, RENEW MY MIND

et's begin with four nuggets of truth to guide us along the way.

First, meditate on these words from Scripture describing *who you are*:

- *If you call Jesus your Lord and Savior, you are a blood-bought daughter of the One True God. Jesus valued you enough to give His life for you and pour out His blood for you. And if you don't know Jesus, I pray you'll meet Him along this journey and come to know Him personally.*
- *You are fully seen, fully known, and fully loved by the One True God.*

Second, let's agree to stand on these two promises from 1 John:

> See what great love the Father has lavished on
> us, that we should be called children of God!
> And that is what we are! (1 John 3:1)

You, dear children, are from God and have overcome them, because the one who is in you is greater than the one who is in the world. (1 John 4:4)

Did you catch the last half of 1 John 4:4? Read it again. *Greater* is the One who lives in you than the one who lives in the world. Friend, we overcome *because* God's very presence—His Holy Spirit—lives, breathes, and is at work in us. God's Spirit in us ensures we're able to overcome the trials, schemes, temptations, and lies of the evil one.

Third, remember that *who* you are never changes, no matter *where* you are. This is true for any emotion that holds you hostage. One of the purposes of *Rest for Your Soul* is to give you the tools you need to change *where* you are, no matter what's holding you captive.

Finally, as children of God, we have promises from God that are ours in Christ. I've placed these promises in the following declaration. Please pray it with me as we begin. Then take a moment to declare the truths out loud over your heart and mind. This may feel a bit awkward, but I promise it will help the promises behind these words soak into your heart and mind.

> *Through the blood of Jesus, I am **redeemed** out of the hand of the devil.*
>
> *Through the blood of Jesus, my sins are **forgiven**, washed white as snow.*
>
> *Through the blood of Jesus, I am **justified**, made righteous in God's eyes, just as if I'd never sinned.*
>
> *Through the blood of Jesus, I am made **holy** in God's sight, set apart for His purposes.*
>
> *Through the blood of Jesus, I receive the gift of, and am **sealed** by, the Holy Spirit, making my body a living, breathing temple of God's Holy Spirit.*
>
> *Through the blood of Jesus and the indwelling power of His Holy*

*Spirit, I am an **overcomer**. Satan has no hold on me. He has no power over me. He must flee at the name of Jesus.*

Friend, these are God's truths from His Word. You may not understand every word you're declaring—and that's okay. You may not feel like an overcomer right now—and that's okay. But what you can know is that when you declare God's Word, He says it will not return to Him empty. It will accomplish what He desires and achieve the purposes for which He sent it (Isaiah 55:11).

These declarations are God-given weapons to fight the Enemy. When you hear Satan whisper *Quit. Give up. This is too hard. It's taking too long. It's asking too much*, go back to these promises. Declare them again and again, as many times as you have to. Write them down. Keep them close. Stand on each one. Remind yourself of your title as God's beloved daughter and the promises that come with that title.

You, daughter, are an overcomer!

Since we're about to embark on a journey that will be steeped in God's Word, my last word of encouragement is about Scripture and comes from one of theology's most treasured voices, A. W. Tozer:

> The Bible is not an end in itself, but a means to bring men to an intimate and satisfying knowledge of God, that they may enter into Him, that they may delight in His Presence, may taste and know the inner sweetness of the very God Himself in the core and center of their hearts.[1]

Let these words tumble around in your heart. Consider each chapter you read as an invitation to delight deeper in God's presence, to taste and know the inner sweetness of God more intimately than ever before.

As we embark on our journey into God's tried-and-true holy habits, two foundational principles come into play:

- Retraining our brains with truth
- Creating a prepared and prayerful heart

First, I'll share why retraining our brains is critical to settling our unsettled souls.

RETRAINING OUR BRAINS WITH TRUTH

Remember how I said I longed to feel "normal" again? By that, I meant I wanted to go back to the place where anxiety, and all that accompanied it, didn't control my life.

But, quite often, our souls feel unsettled and our minds scattered because we're placing our hope in things that will never fully satisfy or bring us rest.

God's Word has taught me that I can't tie my hope to my circumstances. That kind of hope fails every time. Rather, our hope must be tied to God and the unchanging promises sitting in the pages of His Word, in the unwavering belief that He will ultimately bring good from our circumstances, even when it's not the reality we're living.

What I came to learn is that my unsettledness—my anxiety—didn't so much control my life as it controlled my mind. My mind then controlled my thoughts. My thoughts, in turn, controlled my actions. My actions, in turn, controlled my life.

⊘ **What about you? Take a moment to think about what or who controls your thoughts and write what comes to mind.**

List the thoughts most consuming your mind.

_____

_____

_____

_____

_____

_____

How are those thoughts impacting your actions?

_____

_____

_____

_____

_____

_____

How are those actions impacting your life?

_____

_____

_____

_____

_____

_____

Because my problem centered on what controlled my mind, I knew I had to change my mind before God could quiet my heart and still my soul.

I wrote these words in my journal that day:

My goal: Renew my mind.

My how: Retrain my brain to replace the negative thoughts holding it captive and replace those thoughts with the good things of God. Remind myself this will take TIME!

My why: To quiet my heart and still my soul.

Though the heart of this book is retraining our brains spiritually, I would be remiss if I didn't spend some time talking about the science behind retraining our brains. In my studies, I learned that God designed our brains with the ability to do just this.

I did a lot of reading, so I'll summarize what I found relevant to our conversation first, and then share it again in my words and hopefully make it more relatable.

The science behind retraining our brains is called *neuroplasticity. Neuro* refers to neurons, nerve cells that are the building blocks of the brain and nervous system. *Plasticity* refers to the brain's malleability (its capability of being changed by an outside force).[2]

Scientists estimate the human brain is composed of 86 billion neurons. They have also discovered that our brains possess the capacity to reorganize those neurons and the pathways they follow. Our brains can even create new neural connections and, in some cases, create new neurons (neuroplasticity), which enable it to both compensate for, and recover from, physical and emotional injury and trauma.[3]

Here's my translation. *Elohim*, God our wise and all-knowing Creator, designed the human brain to adapt to physical and emotional trauma. God created our brains in such a way that each of us can literally change the brain's physical structure by helping it make new connections through new activities and experiences. Some of the changes will strengthen current connections and eliminate others. Some can even create new neural connections, called sprouting.[4] Why does this matter? Because with faith, prayer, commitment, and hard work, we can "prune" away the connections that are detrimental to our health and create new connections that will lead us into places of wholeness and healing.

It all comes down to identifying what we fix our thoughts on, because what we focus on drives neural connections. Our thoughts throughout the day affect our mood, our behavior, our thinking, our words, and, most importantly, our faith. Our brains tend to run on the same track day in and day out. This means our thoughts will follow the same pathways unless we take action to stop them.

☙ **Where are your thoughts taking you each day? Do you worry about your health? Do you obsess on what others think about you? Do you always assume the worst happening? Do you ruminate on**

past hurts? Do anxious thoughts consume your mind? Does fear control your every waking hour?

If you find yourself obsessing on the same thought patterns, as I did with my anxiety, it's time for some pruning, my friend! Time to replace those thoughts with new ones. Time to create new pathways in your brain and new tracks for your thoughts to follow.

If you're ready, our first step will be learning how to interrupt and redirect our negative, unhealthy recurring thoughts down a new pathway—the pathway of biblical truth.

As we master retraining our brain with God's Truth, our new pathway will replace our old pathway and become the "go-to" pathway for our thoughts.

God's Truth is a powerful weapon to retrain our brains and give us victory over unhealthy thinking.

Let's dive into "the how." How do we retrain our brains with truth?

WE RETRAIN OUR BRAINS BY RENEWING OUR MIND

Walking through the three questions we answered earlier brought this verse to mind:

> Do not conform to the pattern of this world, but be transformed by the renewing of your mind. Then you will be able to test and approve what God's will is—his good, pleasing and perfect will. (Romans 12:2)

I really like reading this same verse in *The Message*:

> So here's what I want you to do, God helping you: Take your everyday, ordinary life—your sleeping, eating, going-to-work, and walking-around life—and place it before God as an offering. Embracing what God does for you is the best thing you can do for him. Don't become so well-adjusted to your culture that you fit into it without even thinking. Instead, fix your attention on God. You'll be changed from the inside out. Readily recognize what he wants from you, and quickly respond to it. Unlike the culture around you, always dragging you down to its level of immaturity, God brings the best out of you, develops well-formed maturity in you. (Romans 12:1–2)

The biblical truth hidden in this verse, which I'm about to dive into, is critically important: **God's Word transforms our minds.**

Take a moment. Read it again and allow it to settle in. It's the foundation upon which this chapter is built.

"Transformed" as used here is from the Greek word *metamorphoó*, which means "to change from one form into another." Specifically, as used here, it means a change of moral character for the better.

When you and I spend more time with God in His Word and less time obsessing on our negative, doubting, anxious thoughts, *that* is when change happens for the better. Being in my Bible—being in our Bibles—anchors our minds in God's Truth. Not our truth, not our parents' truth, not the world's truth. God's Truth.

For me, opening my Bible, even when I didn't feel like it, was an important first step out of my downward spiraling unsettledness. And this decision meant more than reading God's Word and ingesting it (taking it in). It meant digesting it—letting it become a part of who I am. Jeremiah 15:16 says, "When your words came, I ate them; they were my joy and my heart's delight, for I bear your name, LORD God Almighty."

It's only in this surrendered place that God can begin to retrain our brains and renew our minds to think His thoughts—to replace our thoughts with His. God literally changes our minds through His Word.

My friend Shae Tate describes retraining our brains as "reframing" our thoughts. She explains that reframing isn't ignoring our reality or overlooking the hurt or abuse we suffered. Rather, it's choosing to factor God back into the equation, remembering who He is and what's true in the middle of what feels scary and overwhelming.

Reframing our thoughts and retraining our brains is a choice we make to believe God is who He says He is and will do what He says He will do. And that belief then greatly influences our faith.

How? I'm so glad you asked.

Here's another snippet from one of my journals:

The strength of my faith and the measure of my peace directly coincide with the time I spend alone with God.

Read this again, personalizing it for yourself. Friend, you need to know and believe that the strength of your faith and the measure of your peace directly coincides with the time you commit to spend alone with God.

Change came for me when I opened my Bible simply to hear from God personally. Not to teach others. Not to learn theology. But just to be with God. He met me right where I was. He gave me truths I needed to hear and be reminded of—truths and verses I'm going to share with you. Though my verses speak to anxiety, this very same process works with whatever controls your thoughts. Fear. Doubt. Unforgiveness. Bitterness. Betrayal. We'll talk more later about how to find your verses.

Here are my anxiety verses:

Anxiety in the heart of man causes depression,
But a good word makes it glad. (Proverbs 12:25 NKJV)

*Peace I leave with you; my peace I give you.
I do not give to you as the world gives. Do not let your
hearts be troubled and do not be afraid. (John 14:27)*

*You will keep in perfect peace
those whose minds are steadfast,
because they trust in you. (Isaiah 26:3)*

This last verse especially convicted me. It informed me that I played an active role in experiencing the promised perfect peace that is mine in Jesus. First, I had to keep my mind steadfast—fixed on God, not my circumstances. Second, I needed a trusting heart that believed in God's faithfulness.

How do we get that kind of trust and faith? We go again to God's Word for guidance.

His Word tells us to "[b]e still, and know" (Psalm 46:10).

This is where our holy habits of solitude and silence come in.

Let's take a few minutes to study these two words.

Solitude and silence are similar but not the same. They're like cousins.

Both practice *not* doing something. But they practice differently.

As it relates to our journey, solitude creates space for growth. It requires temporarily removing ourselves from people and activities to be present with God.

Henri Nouwen, a beloved pastor, theologian, and one of my favorite authors, says it well: "In solitude I get rid of my scaffolding."[5] This means we step away from what holds us up, what competes for our time, and what feeds our unsettledness. We intentionally set apart time to study Scripture, read a book, listen to worship music, take long walks, or ride a bike.

Later, we'll put solitude into practice by memorizing God's Word together. I can't wait to begin that journey with you!

Silence goes even deeper than solitude. Silence creates inner space to hear God's voice. It's set-apart time to be still and quiet before God . . . alone. In the beginning, silence feels intimidating, even scary. It puts us alone with our thoughts. I didn't want to be alone with my thoughts because when I tried, my bad thoughts and my anxious thoughts always pressed in. They got louder and louder, making me more anxious.

That's why what we're committing to in this book is not a sprint or even a quick run. It's a step-by-step, day-by-day journey.

Henri Nouwen describes silence better than I ever could:

> At first silence might only frighten us. In silence we start hearing voices of darkness: our jealousy and anger, our resentment and desire for revenge, our lust and greed, and our pain over losses, abuses, and rejections. These voices are often noisy and boisterous. They may even deafen us. Our most spontaneous reaction is to run away from them and return to our entertainment.
>
> But if we have the discipline to stay put and not let these dark voices intimidate us, they will gradually lose their strength and recede into the background, creating space for the softer, gentler voices of the light.
>
> These voices speak of peace, kindness, gentleness, goodness, joy, hope, forgiveness, and most of all, love. They might at first seem small and insignificant, and we may have a hard time trusting them. However, they are very persistent and they will be stronger if we keep listening. They come from a very deep place and from very far. They have been speaking to us since before we were born, and they reveal to us that there is no darkness in the One who sent us into the world, only light. They are part of God's voice calling us from all eternity: "My beloved child, my favorite one, my joy."[6]

Nouwen's words should move our hearts to long for holy silence. Silence, when fully engaged in, loosens the grip that dark thoughts and negative voices have on us. It creates space for God to bring in those renewing thoughts that Paul talked about that will transform our minds.

For me, it wasn't until I intentionally committed to times of solitude and silence that I realized how rarely I had experienced either one. I didn't like silence; I used the television as background noise. All day, every day. In fact, one day I glanced over at the TV screen and saw this question: "Are you still watching?" Those words hit me hard. I had numbed my mind to the din of the TV for so long that I didn't even notice what was on or how long it had been on. It was simply background voices filling my head so I wouldn't have to hear my own. I then knew that my first step to disconnecting from the world was to turn off the television unless I was actively watching it.

But it wasn't just background noise. I came to realize that television also kept my mind occupied. It was my escape—I didn't have to think about my anxiety and the symptoms it brought. I watched old movies and television shows. I mean old—ones that my parents and grandparents watched. Their familiarity brought me comfort. And, honestly, they sometimes still do because I know the characters, the episodes, the endings . . . it's a safe space with no surprises.

Over time my escape had become my habit. It centered and calmed me and kept my mind off the thoughts that spiraled me into anxiety.

A habit is a mental, physical, or emotional pattern we've done for so long that we don't even think about it. It takes a long time to break a habit and exchange it for a new one.

We can have good habits and bad habits. My obsessive television watching was not a good habit.

God created me—us—for solitude and silence. We need both.

I spent my time trying to avoid both.

☉ **How much time do you spend in solitude? Remember, solitude is removing yourself from people and things to be present with God and His creation.**

⊘ **What about silence? How often do you set apart time to be still and quiet before God?**

_____

_____

_____

_____

⊘ **What keeps you from setting aside time for solitude and silence?**

_____

_____

_____

_____

⊘ **Based on what we've studied, if you're someone who struggles to make time for solitude and silence, what could solitude and silence look like in your life? And, if you do practice these quiet times with God, what would it look like to go deeper?**

_____

_____

_____

_____

_____

_____

Is there really a difference between solitude and silence? Yes!

Solitude is purposefully and intentionally withdrawing from where you are to go to a quiet place. There may be people around you, but they are not with you.

Solitude creates the space for silence. Silence is purposefully and intentionally dedicating time to be alone, away from people. It might even mean abstaining from speaking.

Both move us to _stop_ doing something.

Both create space to:

- Experience closeness with God
- Prepare our hearts to hear from God
- Settle our souls
- Redirect our thoughts

God calls us to stop and rest, then drink from His sacred well. The crucial question is, how often do you stop and drink from that sacred well to be refreshed and refilled with God's holy, living water?

When do you find time? Rarely? Or, like me, maybe never?

I want to share good news, friend. When I finally decided to drink from that well, I couldn't get enough! Oh, it didn't come easily or quickly. In the beginning, it felt more like a duty; there wasn't much "spiritual" about it. I scheduled time every night before I went to bed to disconnect from everything—to sit or lie quietly alone in my room. Breathing. Resting. Listening. Praising. Pondering. I'll share more about this in a later chapter.

I can't stress or say enough how much we truly need this time. But it is not another thing on our to-do list. It is not something we have to do to earn God's love and approval. It's much better than that. It's an invitation from the God of the universe to spend time with Him. He is the One who created us and loves us more than anyone else on this planet! But, like any invitation we receive, it's our choice whether we accept or reject it, *each and every day.*

JESUS'S INVITATION TO THE WOMAN AT THE WELL

Jesus gave an invitation to the Samaritan woman at the well in John 4:13–15: "Jesus said to her, 'Everyone who drinks of this water will be thirsty again, but whoever drinks of the water that I will give him will never be thirsty again. The water that I will give him will become in him a spring of water welling up to eternal life.' The woman said to him, 'Sir, give me this water, so that I will not be thirsty or have to come here to draw water'" (ESV).

Let's take a few minutes and learn from Jesus.

⊙ **Read John 4:1–42. I know this is a lot of story to read, but I promise that John's words and this woman's story will bless you.**

Have you ever wondered why John specified the time and place where Jesus met this woman? John 4:6 tells us the woman came to the well at noon. It would have been the hottest part of the day, the time when people's thirst is the greatest. Most women in her day gathered at the well early in the morning or late in the day to escape the heat. But Jesus knew He would find her alone because He knew her story. He knew her past. He knew her thirst. She was looking for true love. She had been married five times and was currently living with another man. In her culture, women would have harshly judged another woman with a colored past and a questionable living situation. Scholars believe this woman chose to go in the middle of the day to avoid those women and their judgy eyes.

Yet Jesus saw her. He set this divine appointment before time began. It was an appointment that required He be alone with her so He could minister to her, value her, and shift her eyes off her circumstances and onto Him.

Near the end of their conversation, Jesus told the woman to get her husband. She replied that she had no husband. Jesus's instruction exposed the shameful fact that she had had five husbands and was not married to the man she was currently living with. His statement gives great insight into this woman's heart and her hurt. In Jesus's time, only men could initiate divorce. Jesus's words seem to indicate five men had already left her. Five times rejected. Five times ashamed. Five times left vulnerable and alone.

But, knowing Jesus's heart, I don't believe He did this to call out her sinful living. He spoke this to name her shame, the most painful part of her story. By doing this, He brought healing.

Friend, this story is extraordinarily telling and tender, especially for women. Not only did Jesus meet this woman in the middle of her sin and shame and minister to her, but He honored her. When she talked about the coming Messiah, He said to her: *"I am he"* (v. 26).

Y'all don't miss what I'm about to say next. In the middle of this woman's sin, in the middle of her loneliness and isolation from her community, Jesus openly and publicly acknowledged that He was the Messiah. What makes this epic? Jesus revealed Himself to a woman. Women were not highly valued in Jewish culture. She was a Samaritan, meaning she was not a Jew. Jesus, by His own words, said that He came for the Jews. Yet, going against the culture, Jesus came to her. A shunned woman. A divorced woman. A Samaritan woman!

Why is the fact that she's a Samaritan significant? The Jews had a deep distrust and dislike for the Samaritans due to ethnic, racial, and religious issues. After the Assyrians captured Samaria, some of the surviving Israelites who had not been deported intermarried with the foreigners left in that land. The Israelites called those people "Samaritans" and considered them ceremonially unclean, racially impure, and to be avoided at all costs. For Jesus to associate at all with this unclean, impure woman was shocking. Yet He not only spoke to her but He pursued her and revealed His true identity to her!

Jesus found this woman anchored in cultural and personal shame, met her alone in the heat of the day, engaged her in conversation, and lifted her out of her shame. He filled her. He quenched her thirst. He transformed her life in a way that led her entire village to Him!

Jesus came in her solitude and turned her life around. He turned her mourning to joy and did exactly what Paul said God's words would do. *Jesus transformed her by the renewing of her mind with truth.*

Oh, friend, don't you want moments like that with Jesus? I do! We won't have them if we don't set aside time to be alone with Him. It was an ordinary day. This woman was doing an ordinary task. And, in that quiet place, Jesus came to her in an extraordinary way and changed her life!

Yes, Lord! More of this for me and for my friend!

☞ Sit with this story. Read it again. Now revisit the two questions I asked at the beginning of this book: "What is your soul thirsting for?" and "What wells are you drinking from to fulfill your soul's thirsty places?" What did you answer?

_____

_____

_____

_____

_____

_____

_____

☞ The Samaritan woman's story teaches us that those earthly wells we continually visit will never fully satisfy. Eventually, they will run dry. Thinking of your answers to the two questions just given, ask God to show you what He wants you to take from the woman's meeting with Jesus. Are there specific words that speak to your heart? Convict your heart? Comfort you where you are? Encourage you? Write down what you hear and feel and describe one step you can take to satisfy that thirst in your soul.

_____

_____

_____

_____

_____

_____

_____

WARNING SIGNS WE NEED SOLITUDE AND SILENCE AND FINDING THE ANSWER IN MEDITATING AND RESTING

Our bodies often present warning signs that alert us to our need for solitude and silence. We feel emotions like restlessness. Loneliness. Anxiety. Fear. Depression. I experienced most of these, and that's what alerted me that I needed help. I know now those emotions were direct evidence of a dry and thirsty soul who needed to slow down and receive the fresh fillings of living water that only Jesus can provide.

Oh, friend, please hear me. The more we create time and space to meet with our Creator on a consistent basis, the more we experience Him. The more we experience Him, the more we long to return. That's when our time spent with Him becomes our delight, not our duty.

That time alone with God trains our minds to *meditate on* and *rest in* Him.

Some Christians balk at that word "meditate" because they connect it to Eastern meditation. But meditation by itself is neutral. It's simply quieting your mind.

What's the difference between Christian and Eastern meditation? Christian meditation is a religious practice grounded in God. It invites followers to focus on God and listen for His voice. Christian meditation seeks to fill the mind and transform it.

Eastern and/or secular meditation has no connection to the One True God. It directs followers to listen to their inner self and find their answers from within. Eastern meditation seeks to empty the mind, not fill it.

In John 15:5, Jesus invites us into Christian meditation. He invites us to "abide" (ESV), or "remain" (NIV), in Him. We receive Him in the abiding and remaining. Paul also spoke to abiding in Philippians 4:8, when he invited us to think on "whatever is true, whatever is noble, whatever is right, whatever is pure, whatever is lovely, whatever is admirable—if anything is excellent or praiseworthy—think about such things." Where do we find "such things"? We find them in Scripture.

The holy habits of solitude and silence don't empty us—they *fill* us!

They bring us closer to the heart of God, allow us to hear His voice, and ensure that we receive fresh fillings of His goodness, mercy, grace, wisdom, knowledge, peace, joy, and hope.

Other places in Scripture confirm John 15 and God's desire that we abide in Him and meditate on His Word.

> Keep this Book of the Law always on your lips; meditate on it day and night, so that you may be careful to do everything written in it. Then you will be prosperous and successful. (Joshua 1:8, emphasis added)

> Blessed is the one... whose delight is in the law of the LORD,
>   and who meditates on his law day and night.
> That person is like a tree planted by streams of water,
>   which yields its fruit in season
> and whose leaf does not wither—
>   whatever they do prospers. (Psalm 1:1–3, emphasis added)

When I see the word "meditate" in these two verses, it brings to mind this image of sitting in a quiet place, pondering and reflecting upon the spiritual truth I'm studying. Which is true—that is the English meaning of the word.

However, this word in the original Hebrew language is *hagah* and takes our English definition a bit further. It means "to moan, utter." To ruminate. To eat or chew on something.

We see *hagah* again in Isaiah 31:4: "For thus the LORD said to me, 'As a lion or young lion **growls** over his prey . . .'" (ESV). This time *hagah* is translated as "growl." So, to meditate also means to devour God's Word like a lion eats its prey.

Now, that's a totally different visual for meditating than mine. Right?

Theologian Charles Spurgeon, commenting on Psalm 1:2, says this: "By day he gets little intervals of time to read it, so he steals from his nightly rest moments in which to meditate upon it. Reading reaps the wheat, meditation threshes it, grinds it, and makes it into bread. Reading is like the ox feeding—meditation is digesting when chewing the cud. It is not only reading that does us good, but the soul inwardly feeding on it and digesting it."[7]

Wow! Threshes, grinds, chewing, feeding. These words emote such power, right? With the word *hagah* God invites us to open His Word with great intention, to think on it thoroughly and intentionally, to dive into a verse or passage and wrestle with it. To not just *ingest* it but *digest* it so it becomes a part of who we are. We not only know it, but we believe it, we understand it, and we seek to live it.

Throughout Scripture, in both the Old and New Testaments, God invites us to meditate. We can step outside the chaos and busyness of life to meet and hear from Him.

How do we begin? With baby steps. As we move through this book, we'll engage in specific activities to put into practice what we're learning . . . step by step by step.

Here's a few tips to keep in mind. We'll revisit them later.

- **Resolve in your heart** to commit time to solitude and silence.
- **Make a plan and be diligent** to create these new holy habits.
- **Set apart time.** Choose ahead of time which habits you will choose and what you will do, for how long, and where.
- **Begin.** Just do it. Take one day at a time. It's a journey. What matters most is this first step. Begin.

Remember, each sacred pause makes space for God to settle your soul and draw you close so you can hear His voice and experience His presence. Each pause also redirects your thoughts, retrains your brain, and renews your mind in ways that prune away what is weak, strengthen what is strong, and maybe even sprout new growth in your faith.

I promise that once you accept the invitation, it won't take long for God to meet you and move you in ways you've never imagined.

Is it easy? No. For me, at first, it felt like a duty—something I had to do because of the fruit I knew it would produce. It wasn't always easy to go to my room each night. I knew what faced me—silence. The silence that often ignited my already out-of-control emotions into a raging fire, especially on those days where my battle with anxiety had raged all throughout the day. Escaping into "MeTV" Land sounded so much better. But I knew television was not the healthy choice. It was not the choice that would lead to hope and healing.

Over time, that set-apart time—those sacred pauses at the sacred well—helped me in ways I couldn't have imagined when I first committed to spend that time each night in my room in God's Word.

Discipline turned into delight. Reading God's Word turned into abiding in His Word. Solitude turned to silence.

God's Word became the medicine I took every night before bed.

Why do I use the word "medicine"? Because God compares His Word to medicine that brings healing to our bones and health to our body (Proverbs 3:5–8; 4:20–22).

Doctors prescribe medicine to kill the bad infections and illnesses that have invaded our bodies. God's Word does the same for us spiritually and physically.

> Trust in the LORD with all your heart
> and lean not on your own understanding;
> in all your ways submit to him,
> and he will make your paths straight.
>
> Do not be wise in your own eyes;
> fear the LORD and shun evil.
> This will bring health to your body
> and nourishment to your bones.
> (Proverbs 3:5–8, emphasis added)

> My son, pay attention to what I say;
> turn your ear to my words.
> Do not let them out of your sight,
> keep them within your heart;
> for they are life to those who find them
> and health to one's whole body.
> (Proverbs 4:20–22, emphasis added)

These words are God's written prescription from our Great Physician. He prescribes them for our health and healing, physically and spiritually. There is no more powerful medication on this earth than the living, active, penetrating Word of God. Nothing lifts a worn, weary, worried soul more than God's promises!

Friend, in times of fear and anxiety, depression and loneliness, and doubt and grief, we have a choice. Will we choose Jesus, or will we continue on the path we've chosen, which for me wasn't working? Maybe it isn't working for you, either.

Let's stop here because everything in me wants you to be sitting across from me right now, Bibles open, and this time my freshly baked cinnamon cake (see the appendix section for the recipe) between us. I would cup your face in my hands, look deeply into your eyes, and speak these words to you . . .

You, friend, are reading these words because someone prayed you here. Maybe it's your prayers. Your grandmother's prayers. Your friend's prayers. And, I know, my prayers.

The Lord knows that you know your way isn't working. You're weary. Exhausted. Tired of trying to do this on your own. Tired of asking Him every day to take you back to "normal," but normal never comes. All you want is to be set free from what's holding you captive. And God is the only one who can truly free you!

⟳ **Will you commit with me now to choose to sit at God's feet? Write a prayer telling Him exactly what's on your heart and what you're committing to. Set out the details so you can return to this question and your words when you want to give up.**

_____

_____

_____

_____

_____

Anticipation fills my heart as we take this journey of solitude, silence, and prayer. Together we will move toward a place of healing, freedom, and, best of all, overcoming what holds us captive. And along the way we will gain tools and practices to recognize and interrupt what consumes our thoughts. I pray that the next time these intruders try to rear their ugly heads, you'll be prepared with the truths you need to battle and overcome the Enemy! Your heart and mind will be a treasured storehouse of God's verses, truths, and promises.

I'm closing this section with one final lesson Jesus taught His disciples in John 15:5. Be on alert for what Jesus promises when we abide in Him.

> I am the vine; you are the branches. If you remain
> in me and I in you, you will bear much fruit.

The promised gift of abiding is fruit. Not just fruit. _Much_ fruit.

What fruit is Jesus talking about? It's the fruit of His Spirit. What is the fruit of His Spirit? Love, joy, peace, patience, kindness, goodness, faithfulness, gentleness, and self-control (Galatians 5:22–23 ESV).

Friend, the longer we linger with Jesus, the more fruit we bear.

Stay attached! It doesn't take work to stay attached—you just need to keep hanging with Jesus. Drinking His living water from the sacred well. Filling your minds with God's Word, His truth, and His promises. And, most of all, keeping close to His heart through solitude, silence, and prayer.

It's a simple formula.

Show up.

Hold on.

Receive.

He produces the fruit!

CREATING A PREPARED AND PRAYERFUL HEART

We've talked about retraining our brains with truth. That's what helped me address the thoughts that filled my mind, but I also needed to address my heart because the thoughts that controlled my mind also controlled my heart. Anxious thoughts lead to an anxious heart. Fearful thoughts lead to a fearful heart. Chaotic thoughts lead to a chaotic heart.

Now we'll dive into why creating a prepared and prayerful heart is also critical to settling our unsettled souls.

⟡ **Take a few minutes and think about what's happening in your body. Physically, do you experience a racing heart rate? Do you feel like you can't catch your breath when your thoughts overwhelm you? Does it feel like a motor is always running within you? These are symptoms of an overwhelmed body that often lead to an overwhelmed heart. Write any and all physical symptoms you feel in the following lines.**

_____

_____

_____

_____

_____

☙ **Now take time again to think about what's going on in your heart spiritually. Does it, too, feel overwhelmed? Held captive, controlled by your emotions? Never at peace? Consumed with fear? Alone and forgotten? Isolated and hopeless? Describe as best you can the state of your heart spiritually.**

_____

_____

_____

_____

_____

I desperately needed to find a way to prevent my heart from following what was going on in my mind and my body.

I did what I've learned to do—go to God's Word. I searched for a verse that could help me calm my anxious heart. I found this verse on anxiety:

Cast all your anxiety on him because he cares for you. (1 Peter 5:7)

Casting is an intentional act to relocate an object—to move it from one place to another. In this verse, Peter tells us to cast—transfer our unsettledness—from our heart to God's. He becomes our burden bearer.

And, guess what? What Peter was really talking about when he told us to cast our anxiety on Jesus is prayer. Casting the unsettledness in our hearts onto God's is simply another way of telling us to pray.

Prayer is easy for some, but hard for others. We'll delve deeper into prayer in a later chapter. For now, we'll be simple.

How do we pray?

- **Identify what your heart feels.** Guess what? You already answered this in the questions I just shared. Examples might be anxiety, fear, dread, unforgiveness, hopelessness, and bitterness.

- **Tell God what you're feeling.** A simple prayer is all you need. Here are a few ideas to help get you started.

> *Lord, Your Word tells me to cast my (anxiety/fear/hopelessness) on You. It tells me You care for me. So, I'm honoring Your Word and coming to You. Please help me now. I need You.*

> Or

> *Lord, I'm in such a hard place. My head keeps telling me to worry and try to fix this. Nothing changes. My heart feels overwhelmed and consumed. I'm choosing to fully give _____ to You. I know You can carry this for me and resolve it the way You see best. I trust You. Hold me close as we walk the rest of the way together.*

- **Find a specific promise in God's Word that fits your problem.** I'll share how to do just that soon.

Let's go back to one of the verses I shared earlier:

> You will keep in perfect peace
> those whose minds are steadfast,
> because they trust in you. (Isaiah 26:3)

For me, one of the worst things about living with anxiety was my panic attacks. My anxiety always made me feel like I had a motor continuously running in my body, and during my panic attacks that motor revved up to full speed.

Panic attacks turn all of our attention inward. I constantly monitored my feelings, and it was hard to focus on anything else, especially God. I asked the same questions and repeated the same thoughts over and over.

God, will I ever feel normal again? I'm scared. I feel so alone. No one understands. Will these anxious feelings ever go away?

I remember many hard days sitting on my back porch, tears streaming down my face, overwhelmed by this constant script that played in my mind.

When we give permission for those questions and thoughts to invade and remain, they only inflame the out-of-control emotions we already feel. When we don't interrupt them and take steps to kick them out, they make themselves at home in our hearts and plant deep roots.

I suffered through many distressing panic attacks on my back porch. And those attacks only led to more concerns and questions.

I can't keep doing this. Please don't let there be another one. I feel like I can't breathe. Heart, please stop pounding. Motor, please stop running. God, will this ever stop? God, where are you?

Though I'm about to take a deeper dive into panic attacks, the practical tools I'm sharing will apply to any time your mind and body feel out of sorts. It may be obsessive thinking, or it may be irrational thoughts fueled by fear and/or anxiety. You can tweak these tools to work for what you're feeling and experiencing.

Panic attacks often feel similar to what I imagine a heart attack feels like. Your body feels out of control. You can't breathe. Your heart races. You begin to tremble and shake. You may even sweat.

My Isaiah verse came into play most profoundly when my anxiety worsened to the point that I experienced attacks on a daily basis. They took me to a dark place because I had no control over them. I never knew when they would come. It's one reason I didn't want to leave my house.

Friend, I want to stop here for a moment and breathe. This is hard. Going back to those days of repeated panic attacks is difficult because there were days I felt hopeless. Days I believed would never end. Are you there now? I feel like you might be. I want you to know and hear me say, "I'm so sorry. I understand." I have tears in my eyes as I type this. I remember.

You might be thinking, "This is easy for her—she's on the other side." But it's not. I want to share three things before we move on.

First, know you are not alone. Though I suffered mainly panic attacks, any out-of-control feelings, fueled by fear and anxiety, lead us to feel alone and isolated. I truly understand. I've been there, and I'm praying for you right now.

The prayers I'm praying for you today don't go away—they stay with God. God stores these prayers in heaven. You sitting here with me now, reading both these words and God's Word, shows that your prayers are being answered right now. God sees you. He hears you. He brought you here to receive His Word and to learn to pray His Word into your anxiety and fear.

Second, please know that these attacks, these out-of-control feelings, don't mean that you're weak or are a failure. We're human and live in a fallen world. We will feel overwhelmed. We will experience anxiety and fear. Yet what we're walking through is nothing to be ashamed of. It doesn't mean your faith is weak—you will always live like this.

Third, these emotions are manageable.

How?

First, we'll get practical and then we'll get spiritual. And, guess what? We've already been working on the spiritual! So, be encouraged.

Practically, as you feel a panic attack (or obsessive thinking) coming on, don't try to fight it. Breathe. In and out. Deep breaths.

My friend Leah, who graciously and lovingly walked with me on my worst days, gave me this wisdom, and I still use it today. When you feel your emotions rush in at full speed, let them wash over you like a wave rolls over you in the ocean. Don't fight them—fighting makes it worse. Ride the wave all the way through. And trust God through it.

Someone I dearly love, who also struggles with anxiety, shared that he managed his panic attacks by refocusing his thoughts. He refocused by actively thinking and listening to what he saw and felt around him. He looked at what he was wearing, piece by piece, where he was sitting, and what was around him. His redirected thinking calmed his heart and took his mind off the anxiety and panic welling up within him.

Spiritually, what does it look like to trust God through your out-of-control emotions? It helps to find a Bible verse to declare over your heart and mind as you ride that wave and press through your panic. Mine was, and still is, Isaiah 26:3.

We'll talk more about how to find your verse and turn it into a prayer in a later chapter. Here's the CliffsNotes version: identify the trigger/thought that brings on your anxiety/fear/panic attack. Then pray your verse into that trigger or thought. That verse and your prayer interrupt the thoughts consuming your mind and replace them with God's thoughts.

Here's my Isaiah 26:3–4 prayer:

Thank You, God, that You will keep me in Your perfect peace because I am trusting in You and keeping my eyes fixed on you. I will trust You forever, Lord. You are my rock eternal.

Now let's put these steps together.

For me, as I rode the wave of my panic attack, I would first take some deep breaths (from deep in my belly) and then I would pray this prayer until I rode that wave to the other side. I repeated this breathing and praying until the panic subsided.

Rather than pushing against and fighting the emotions consuming you, this training calms your heart as it interrupts and replaces the negative, fearful, hopeless thoughts with God's thoughts.

Breathing, riding, and praying made my panic attacks much more manageable. And over time the attacks lessened in length, strength, and number.

If you're in that place today, friend, surrender. Surrender your feelings and emotions to the only One who can help you defeat, control, and overcome them.

☞ **Now it's your turn. Prayerfully walk through the process we learned. Put it into practice in the space below. Put all the steps together. Identify your emotions. Find your verse. Turn your verse into a prayer. Pray your verse. Then, with each and every thought, pray your prayer. If you're not sure how to find your verse, we'll study this in a later chapter so you can put this into practice at that time.**

_____

_____

_____

_____

_____

Let me close with these crucial words: don't buy into the Enemy's lie that you have to be strong or that you have to be in control at all times.

You don't have to be strong. You don't have to be in control.

God makes it very clear in His Word. There are times when it's good to be weak. Broken. Fragile. Weary.

These are not my words, friend. These are God's words to Paul when he was in a very hard place.

Paul said in 2 Corinthians 12:8–10:

Three times I [Paul] pleaded with the Lord to take it away from me. But [the Lord] said to me, "My grace is sufficient for you, for my power is made perfect in weakness." Therefore I will boast all the more gladly about my weaknesses, so that Christ's power may rest on me. That is why, for Christ's sake, I delight in weaknesses, in insults, in hardships, in persecutions, in difficulties. For when I am weak, then I am strong.

Scripture tells us Paul had an unidentified "thorn" in his side. What was it? A physical weakness? A health issue? A mental issue? We don't know. I believe God intentionally left the specifics out so that His words to Paul apply also to us, no matter what we're suffering.

Take comfort in these words from your Father in heaven: "My grace is sufficient for you, my child, because when you are weak, I am strong." Daughter, God teaches dependency and humility in that place of weakness. And in that surrendered place of dependence and humility, He will shift something deep within you to do a new thing. As my counselor Rebecca says, it's a good thing that will be a better thing.

Nearly every day since I've come out of the other side of the worst of my anxiety, I've spent time in God's Word. Some days are shorter than others. And how I spend my time may vary. It might be in the Bible, a devotional, or in Scripture I'm memorizing.

I'm not going to tell you that I never experience anxiety and my life is perfect. Because it isn't. I still struggle with anxious feelings at times. And most of us will, because of the culture and world we live in.

But because of the commitment I've made and because of the intentional holy habits I've developed, those desperate places of fear and anxiety stay at bay.

Why?

I commit to times of solitude and silence.

I remember that in God's presence are peace and rest!

I continue to retrain my brain and renew my mind.

I resolve to have a prepared and prayerful heart.

LORD, QUIET MY HEART

Have you ever paused to think about what you think about? My counselor invited me to do just that. She invited me to take an inventory of my thoughts about what counselors and psychologists call "mental chatter." She asked me to honestly record my naturally recurring thoughts for one week.

I considered questions like:

- What are my first thoughts in the morning? My last thoughts before I go to bed?

  _____

  _____

- What do I think about most during the day?

  _____

  _____

- Do I see any patterns in those thoughts?

  _____

  _____

- Do my thoughts depend on my location? The people I'm with? The activity I'm engaged in?

  _____

  _____

- What emotions or physical reactions accompany those thoughts?

  _____

  _____

- Are my thoughts negative? Shaming? Doubting? Fear-inducing? Anxiety-producing?

  _____

  _____

What I discovered disturbed me because my answers revealed that anxiety-producing thoughts consumed my mind. All. Day. Long. Now, Rebecca didn't invite me into this exercise to induce fear and increase my anxiety. She knew that completing the exercise would provide valuable information I needed to know for my next steps because I couldn't change what I didn't know.

The results of my thoughts inventory confirmed that I desperately needed to quiet my mind. This is where I committed to my first holy habit and my first sacred pause—solitude. I set apart time in my day to sit quietly with God in His Word.

Friend, when we find ourselves here, where we don't know the answers, we need to do the only thing we can do—put one foot in front of the other and walk. Step by step. The path we travel may feel messy, frustrating, confusing, dark, and even lonely. God is okay with that. Oftentimes, this is where He does His best work.

Jesus walked step by step with His Father during one of His darkest times. He took a sacred pause in the garden of Gethsemane just before He went to the cross. Initially we see Him in great distress, praying desperate prayers about His Father's plan for Him (Mark 14:36). In the end, Jesus traded His will for His Father's, fully placing His hope and future in Him. Aren't we grateful for that sacred pause?

↻ **Take a few minutes to complete your thoughts inventory.**

_____

_____

_____

↻ **What did you discover?**

_____

_____

_____

↻ **What do you want your next step to be?**

_____

_____

_____

Write a prayer and ask God to help you take that next step.

_____

_____

_____

_____

_____

_____

_____

SOLITUDE: SACRED PAUSES WITH GOD

Be encouraged as we walk into this solitude journey. You can trust we're on the right track because the choices we're making are the very same ones we saw Jesus model and prioritize in His life.

Let's open God's Word to find where Jesus chose sacred pauses and where He invited His disciples into the same.

⟋ **Read Matthew 14:13–23. After Jesus fed the five thousand, what did He do?**

_____

_____

_____

_____

⟋ **Why do you think Jesus desired solitude after feeding the five thousand? This is one of only a few times in Matthew's gospel that he references Jesus praying. Why do you think Matthew included this part of the story?**

_____

_____

_____

_____

_____

Mark's gospel provides another example of Jesus entering into a time of solitude.

Not long after Jesus fed the five thousand, He dismissed the crowd and asked His disciples to go ahead of Him. Matthew tells us that Jesus then withdrew and "went up on the mountain by himself to pray. When evening came, he was there alone" (Matthew 14:23 ESV).

After a full day of teaching, healing, and driving out demons in Capernaum, Scripture tells us that Jesus intentionally chose to get up early and "while it was still dark, he departed and went out to a desolate place, and there he prayed" (Mark 1:35 ESV).

Let's spend time examining a few more of Jesus's sacred pauses and look for the "why." Scripture provides great insight when we consider each sacred pause in light of what was happening around Jesus.

SACRED PAUSES PREPARE AND SUSTAIN US FOR WILDERNESS TIMES AND SPIRITUAL BATTLES

☙ **Read Luke 3:21–22.** Imagine you're on the riverbank observing this historical biblical moment. Consider every detail. What do you feel? Ponder what Jesus would have felt. How do you think this encounter with His Father impacted Jesus mentally, physically, and spiritually, knowing He was about to begin three years of ministry?

_____

_____

_____

_____

_____

☙ **Now read Luke 4:1–2.** According to verse 1, where did the Spirit lead Jesus? Who would He encounter there?

_____

_____

_____

☙ How did Jesus's baptism prepare Him for this forty-day battle with the devil?

_____

_____

_____

God had gone before His Son. God knew the physical and spiritual battle that lay ahead for Jesus, so He prearranged for John to baptize Jesus and infuse Him with a fresh filling of the Holy Spirit's power. Jesus's baptism ensured that He entered into the forty-day wilderness time "full of the Holy Spirit" (Luke 4:1).

Scripture tells us that the Spirit led Jesus into solitude. For nearly six weeks, Jesus withdrew from family, friends, and crowds to spend time in the wilderness with His Father. It was both a physical and a spiritual wilderness. During those forty days, He engaged in some serious spiritual warfare with the devil. And what's so beautiful is that God provided all Jesus needed through His Word (Matthew 4:1–11).

When we encounter God's people in the wilderness, we consistently see God's provision. Whether it was in the mountains, the deserts, or the high seas, God provided strength, healing, protection, direction, redirection, hope, and much more. In their uncomfortable and painful adversity, God's people learned to trust Him more deeply and fully through His presence and provision.

We also find God's protection and redirection in the midst of spiritual battles. We see this come alive as we travel with Joseph from the pit, where one of his brothers took compassion on him and saved his life. We go to Egypt, where God gave Joseph favor in Potiphar's eyes. Then to prison, where God gave Joseph favor with the warden. Finally, we come before Pharaoh, where God enabled Joseph to interpret his dreams. These divine, solitude-soaked wilderness times eventually elevated Joseph to the second highest position in Egypt. Through each trial, God protected and redirected Joseph . . . from the pit to the prison to the palace!

No matter how unsafe, uncomfortable, and frightening the wilderness might feel, by its very nature it creates space for solitude, silence, and prayer. It's often God's divine appointment to provide, protect, and redirect us.

With this context around our Luke passage, I think you'll agree solitude is an essential ingredient in preparing and sustaining us for our own spiritual wildernesses.

Sacred Pauses Create Space for Us to Rest, Refill, and Renew

☞ **Read Mark 6:7–13. What action did Jesus take here with regard to the twelve disciples?**

_____

_____

_____

The disciples obeyed Jesus's call to go out among the people. Mark tells us they went out and preached, cast out demons, and anointed and healed the sick. They then returned to Jesus to report all they had done and taught.

⟲ **Read Mark 6:30–32. Knowing the work they had done, what did Jesus tell the disciples to do? Why do you think Jesus instructed them to go to a quiet place?**

_____

_____

_____

_____

I think Jesus sensed the disciples' weariness and knew the best medicine was a sacred pause—a time to rest, refill, and renew. Jesus also knew what was about to happen. A hungry, needy crowd was about to overwhelm them and demand their time and attention.

Sacred Pauses Provide Time to Process Grief and Loss

⟲ **Just after Jesus heard the news of John the Baptist's beheading, what does Matthew 14:13 tell us He did?**

_____

_____

_____

_____

Matthew tells us that Jesus took a sacred pause. We aren't specifically told why He took that pause. Perhaps He spent that time grieving the loss of the one who leapt in his mother Elizabeth's womb when Jesus (still in Mary's womb) came into his presence. Take a moment to read that beautiful story (Luke 1:39–45). Jesus lost a faithful friend and follower that day, the one who had prepared the way for His coming and baptized Him. He needed to take time to grieve.

Sacred Pauses Allow Time to Pray and Seek God's Will in Making Decisions

⟲ <u>Read Luke 6:12–14.</u> What did Jesus do the night before He chose and called His disciples?

_____

_____

_____

Jesus found Himself at a critical point in His ministry. His rejection of the religious leaders' ways and their politics made Him the target of much hatred and persecution. Because of this, Jesus knew the time had come to choose followers who would carry on the work He had done and would continue to do. They would take His Word and His work into the world.

Did you notice that even though Jesus was God, He prayed for wisdom? He didn't simply pull names out of the air or call upon His own infinite knowledge to obtain these names. Luke tells us He prayed—all night. He sought each name from His Father. Why? Because although Jesus was divine, He was also a human. He was one of us. In this situation, Jesus needed to seek the will of His Father and rely on the wisdom of the Spirit—just like us.

Friend, Jesus's example should give us great encouragement. If Jesus needed times of solitude and prayer when seeking God's will, how much more do we?

Sacred Pauses Help Us Find Strength and Resolve as We Wrestle with God about Our Trials and Struggles

⟲ <u>Read Matthew 26:36–45.</u> Reread verse 38. How did Jesus describe His emotional state to His disciples?

_____

_____

_____

_____

Friend, this moment, more than any other in Scripture, displays Jesus's humanity. It is His human side, which God so graciously shows us to encourage us on our journey: "My soul is overwhelmed with sorrow to the point of death" (Matthew 26:38).

John Piper, theologian and scholar, shares his wisdom on this verse:

> This is very dangerous for his mission. It is possible to become so sad, so heavy, that reality is distorted, the future seems hopeless, and action seems impossible. Perhaps you have tasted this. This is not small. Jesus's mission is in jeopardy. He must fight against the immobilizing effects of this horrible weight of sorrow.
>
> He fights by crying out for help to his Father in heaven. Matthew 26:39, "My Father, if it be possible, let this cup pass from me; nevertheless, not as I will, but as you will." The cup would be all the horrors of the next eighteen hours—the physical torture, the abandonment of his friends, the turning away of his Father while he becomes sin for us.[1]

Jesus asked His Father if there was another way to achieve His purpose of salvation other than drinking that cup. If there was, He asked that God let the cup pass without His drinking from it.

Oh, friend, have you been there? That place of deep physical and/or spiritual suffering, unfair persecution, betrayal, and abandonment by those you love. Where darkness surrounds you. Hope eludes you. Despair overwhelms you.

Jesus withdrew deeper into the garden to pray and receive strength in His time of deep distress, processing His agony as He surrendered His will to His Father's.

Jesus again models that solitude is our answer—slipping away to a quiet place to wrestle through our emotions. We do not wrestle alone, but with God. We spill out our every emotion before the Lord—even those feelings that we think will offend Him (don't worry, because they won't).

David set a similar example in Psalm 13.

◌ **Read Psalm 13.** **What phrase does David repeat four times in the first two verses?**

_____

_____

_____

I don't know about you, but this psalm brings me peace and great hope. Even David, the one God called "a man after his own heart" (1 Samuel 13:14), cried out in desperation. He felt forgotten by God. Unseen by God. He grew weary of wrestling with his thoughts and the sorrow that filled his heart.

◌ **How many times have you uttered those or similar words? What circumstances led to this cry in your heart?**

_____

_____

_____

I carried this cry in my heart for over a decade when I battled fear after being raped at age twenty-one by an armed, masked man hiding in my apartment. I cried again as I battled severe anxiety. I continue to utter cries today for a broken relationship in my life.

I truly believe this is the most critical question we ask in our wrestling, because the longer the battle is, the more it feels we cannot endure. We feel God is asking too much of us for too long.

Or we might bargain with God: _God, if only you would tell me how long, then I could endure better._

Waiting is hard. Waiting when it feels like God's distancing Himself from us is even harder because it seems like we don't matter to God. That, of course, is a lie from the Enemy. He is the one who wants us to doubt God's love. His presence. His faithfulness. His goodness.

Of course, God never forgot David in the wilderness. God never forgot Jesus in the garden. And God never forgets us.

It only *feels* like He has forgotten us. It's true according to our feelings but not according to fact. Indeed, our lying feelings create a reality that we will continue to believe and live if we don't step outside our heads and into His Word.

This is where solitude comes in. To prevent our feelings from ruling our thoughts, we need to ensure something else takes charge of those thoughts. We need to retrain our brains by renewing our minds. Sound familiar?

David's psalm helped retrain his brain and renew his mind. He did this often in his psalms. He cried out to God with what was on his heart, even to the point of calling down God's wrath on his enemies. Yet David always came back to Truth. This Truth reminded him that God was not distant. God had not forgotten him. God heard him. God loved him. God was with him. God would help him.

☙ **Do you need help remembering these promises in your wrestling? You'll find Scriptures in the following list to speak to the Enemy when he slithers in with his doubts and his lies. Read each one. Choose one that connects with your heart. Commit to retrain your brain with that verse. Write it on a piece of paper or type it into the notes in your phone so you'll have it on hand when you need it. I encourage you to even try to memorize it (we'll learn about this holy habit in the next chapter). Soon, retraining your brain with this verse will renew your mind and defeat that lie.**

God loves me (Jeremiah 31:3).

God hears me (1 John 5:13–14).

God will help me (Isaiah 41:10).

_____

_____

_____

God is with me (Isaiah 43:2).

_____

_____

_____

God has not forgotten me (Isaiah 49:15).

_____

_____

_____

We've spent time learning the importance of solitude. Now it's time to weave this holy habit of solitude into your everyday life.

One of the best ways to do this is by hiding God's Word in your heart through memorizing Scripture.

THE HOLY HABIT OF HIDING GOD'S WORD IN OUR HEARTS

I can't wait to begin this memorization journey with you! You'll find twelve verses (plus a bonus verse) to memorize at your own pace. At your own pace means you can memorize one verse a week, one verse every other week, or one verse a month. A mini-teaching accompanies each verse to provide context and bring deeper meaning as you learn the verse. I also share memory tools, tips, and words of encouragement along the way.

Before we begin, I'll share a few stories that I hope will encourage you. Last year, I invited friends to join me on social media to memorize seven Scriptures, one each week. We called it the "His Word in My Heart Challenge." On the first day, many women expressed great hesitation as they began. I thought I'd share a few of their comments:

I'm the worst at memorizing anything!

Whenever I've tried in the past, I never stick with it—and I hate that.

I'm afraid I'm too old to memorize Scripture. Nothing sticks.

I have a hard time memorizing word for word.

I feel like my brain can't memorize, but with the guidance and teachings, I really want to try.

Sound familiar? Do you have similar thoughts? You're not alone. I had them too at first.

Now I want to share the great news! God-glorifying news! Many of those women not only accepted the invitation, but they completed all seven weeks despite their initial hesitations and fears. Their comments on the *other side* of our challenge (seven verses later!) brought tears to my eyes. I'm sharing some of my favorite comments, and pray they encourage you as you begin. The first one is my favorite!

Thank you for the "just right" verses God is laying on your heart for us to learn. I'm loving the process. I'm beginning to see each week: Excited to see the new verse, working several days to just remember how the verse starts, getting the meaning of it down, starting to really think about it and apply it to my life **as it gets comfortable inside of me,** holding myself accountable to trying to perfect the words, and then **finally feeling the verse** as it comes to remembrance (even if it's not perfect) because it's now hidden in my heart as the Living Word. So, if any of you have struggled in the process like I have, don't give up!

You can do it. I know each week will be hard. It will take some work, but the internal reward is ETERNAL! Keep sharing your encouragement, friends. It uplifts my spirit.

Thank you for this challenge. I have enjoyed memorizing God's Word, especially since I thought I couldn't do it before I began! I know God has just begun a new work in me, and I will commit to continuing!

Thank you. This journey was so good for me. I said I was having a problem retaining anything . . . yes, I even blamed my age . . . but I found that concentrating on one verse at a time, breaking it down, and writing it turned things around for me.

Sometimes I didn't feel like I was really getting a verse, and I would lie in bed at night trying to recall it. It would come back to me the more I concentrated—the more I recalled the meaning and intent of the Scripture and attended to it . . . and then after it was solid in my brain and present in my heart, I was able to use it to act and apply in my real life. That's been the most amazing and meaningful part.

Though memorizing was pretty hard for me, it was totally worth every effort. The most meaningful time was when I started to go through the verses when I woke up in the middle of the night and couldn't fall back to sleep. The verses helped so much!

Many of the women also enjoyed, and put into practice, tips I shared along the way. So I will share those same tips with you during our journey.

And to add a bit more encouragement, I just finished memorizing my fiftieth verse! My goal was to memorize one verse each week of 2021. It's now July of 2022, so it took me quite a bit longer than I thought. But that's okay, because it's not about being perfect; it's about progress!

A Few Tips on How to Memorize Your Verse

First, write the full verse. Write it in a notebook, on notecards, or in a journal.

Second, learn your verse phrase by phrase. For example, if your verse is 1 John 3:1, break it up into four phrases like this: "See what great love the Father has lavished on us," "that we should be called children of God!" "And that is what we are!" and, finally, "The reason the world does not know us is that it did not know him."

Third, recite your first phrase until you have it in your heart as best as you can, then move to your next phrase. Recite the second phrase, always reciting the first phrase with it. Once you feel comfortable with the first two phrases, add more phrases, always repeating the previous phrases with them.

Fourth, continue to write your verse throughout the week. If you skip a day, no worries . . . grace, grace, always grace!

Sometimes the hardest part of Scripture memory is getting started. At least, that's how it is for me. It's like I have a brain freeze. I remember later phrases, but I can't remember the first phrase for anything! Circling the words that I struggle to remember helps me overcome my brain freeze.

Earlier this year, I memorized Psalm 62:1–2: "Truly my soul finds rest in God; my salvation comes from him. Truly he is my rock and my salvation; he is my fortress, I will never be shaken." Oh, how I struggled to remember that first phrase, "Truly my soul finds rest in God," to get me started. So I circled the first three words, "Truly my soul." I repeated them over and over again before I went into the rest of the verse, whether writing or speaking it. The visual of the circles around the words really helped me remember them. It's been many months, and every now and then I may forget those first few words. But I don't let this frustrate me or cause me to give up, because I know they will eventually come.

Memorization takes patience and repetition. But we can be assured we're doing exactly what God calls us to do because Psalm 119:11 encourages us to hide God's Word in our hearts. We can know that if this is God's desire, He will not only help us but He will bless our obedience.

Below you'll find twelve memory verses, each with its own mini-teaching.

If you're reading this book with friends in a study, you may decide to choose one verse to memorize together for the week, and then once you finish the book you can memorize the remainder of the verses. If you're reading this book on your own, you might decide to pause in this chapter, spend the next few weeks memorizing the twelve verses, and then pick the book back up when you've completed your memorization and head into the next chapter. It's really up to you and what works best for you.

MEMORY VERSES

Psalm 16:8

> I have set the Lord always before me;
> because he is at my right hand, I shall
> not be shaken. (ESV)

What quickened my heart as I read this verse is the author King David's word choice: "*I have set* the Lord always before me." David made a conscious, intentional decision to put God constantly in view. He predetermined to process all he saw and experienced through this perspective.

Luke translated these same words in Acts 2:25 (ESV), using the word "saw" instead of "set." How I love this: "I saw the Lord always before me." That's a powerful image and one that gives me great confidence, because when we have set—when we see the Lord—always before us, we need not be shaken. That word "shaken" is *mot* in Hebrew and means "to totter, to shake, to slip." Keeping the Lord ever before us ensures we stand firm and secure in Him.

The secret of deep and abiding joy, peace, and security is living in the presence of our Lord each and every day—seeing His face ever before us, comforting, guiding, leading, teaching, defending, holding, and protecting us.

☞ **What's one step you can take to set the Lord before you today?**

_____

_____

_____

_____

_____

_____

_____

_____

_____

Tip

You've hidden your first verse in your heart. Congratulations! This is hard stuff, especially for those of us who struggle with memorization.

It may feel harder as we add more verses. Here's another tip. At least four or five times a week, write and recite the *prior* weeks' verses *before* you write/recite your verse for the current week. Recite each verse one after the other several times. Write them in your journal/notebook or on your notecards. Circle the words you struggle remembering.

It also helps me to recite my verses (one after the other) in the morning before I jump out of bed and as I lay my head on my pillow at night. It only takes a few minutes and keeps them fresh in your mind, ready to recall anytime you need them.

Following these tips three to five days a week helps ensure your verse stays hidden in your heart. Even if you mix up words, it's okay! Keep pressing on. Don't give up or quit. It's not about being perfect; it's about progress. Remember, you have the Holy Spirit to teach and remind you, and you can do all things through Christ who strengthens you!

Isaiah 26:3-4

> You will keep in perfect peace
> those whose minds are steadfast,
> because they trust in you.
> Trust in the LORD forever,
> for the LORD, the LORD himself, is the Rock eternal.

When my anxiety was at its worst, I longed to go back to the time before my uncontrollable emotions took control of my life.

As I wrestled through my anxiety, God gave me these three words: Change your position.

Why? I'm sure it's because, as I shared earlier, night after night I binge-watched Netflix and old movies, trying to escape my reality. But one night, something changed. That night, I made the intentional decision to put into action what I had heard from God. I "changed" my position, both physically and mentally. Each night, I now went upstairs to my room and read my Bible. God used this holy time, this holy habit, to renew my mind and remind me of who He was and of what He had done for me in the past. I had no agenda except to listen. I read and wrote my thoughts down in a journal. That time with the Lord led to a treasury of Bible verses, many of which I'm sharing with you now. Truths, promises, and principles from God gave me a new lens through which I could defeat my anxiety.

This verse from Isaiah 26:3 rose to the top of those treasured verses. I personalized the verse and prayed it every day, many times a day.

Thank You, Father, that peace, the fruit of Your Spirit, lives in me. Thank You for Your promise that You will keep me in perfect peace when I trust in You and keep my eyes fixed on You. Today, I commit to trust in You and keep my eyes fixed not on my anxious thoughts but on You, so that Your peace will reign and rule in my heart. In Jesus's name I pray, amen.

I continue to pray this verse every morning before I get out of bed, keeping my eyes fixed on the peace that is mine in Christ.

🖝 **Find a verse that speaks into your situation. Personalize it and pray it each day.**

_____

_____

_____

Word of Encouragement

More to celebrate! You now have two verses hidden in your heart. I'm so very proud of you. This isn't easy. Are you ready for number three?

Colossians 3:12-13

Therefore, as God's chosen people, holy and dearly loved, clothe yourselves with compassion, kindness, humility, gentleness and patience. Bear with each other and forgive one another if any of you has a grievance against someone. Forgive as the Lord forgave you.

To better understand this memory verse, let's travel up to the verses preceding it (specifically verses 9 and 10) where Paul talked about "taking off" our old selves and "putting on" our new selves. The moment we accept Jesus as our Lord and Savior, the old, unbelieving flesh part of us died. Jesus then gave us a new spirit, His Holy Spirit, to live in us.

This beautiful new birth began a new life in us. It is a life where God continually renews us day by day as we seek to love, obey, and reflect Him to our world.

Our first verse (12) begins, "Therefore." This word signals that because of the miraculous work God has done in verses 9 and 10, we have a new identity. We are now His children.

How do we reflect Jesus to the world? By living fully in the fruit of the Holy Spirit who is in us. By being a willing vessel God can use to showcase His compassion, kindness, humility, gentleness, patience, and forgiveness to those around us.

These are not just words we read. They're an invitation—an invitation to live these words out in our everyday, walking-around lives.

⊘ **Will you join me this week in praying for opportunities to live out the fruit that fills you? Come back and note the opportunities God gave you, what happened, and how you felt.**

_____

_____

_____

_____

Abba Father, I invite You to do a mighty work in me as I commit to "put on" my new self in tangible ways. Take what I'm hiding in my heart and create opportunities for me to live it out wherever You lead me. I am willing, Lord. I want to shine Your light and love. I ask this in Jesus's name, amen.

Word of Encouragement

As we continue our Scripture memory journey, I pray these excerpts from Psalm 1 encourage you when the evil one whispers, "This is too hard, just give up."

Blessed is the one whose . . . delight is in the law of the Lord, *and on his law she meditates day and night. She is like a tree planted by streams of water that yields its fruit in season, and whose leaf does not wither. Whatever she does prospers (Psalm 1:1–6).*

Friend, let's delight in the law of the Lord. Let's not give up meditating on it day and night. For when we do, we will be prosperous. Fruitful fountains of living water will fill us and overflow from us so we can then bless and encourage others.

Hebrews 1:3

*The Son is the radiance of God's glory and the exact
representation of his being, sustaining all things by his
powerful word. After he had provided purification for sins,
he sat down at the right hand of the Majesty in heaven.*

Hebrews 1:3 reveals three attributes of Jesus. First, Jesus radiates God's glory. What does this glory look like? Picture the warmth and beauty of the sun's rays on a clear day. Nothing separates the rays from the sun. When you see one, you see the other. That's how the Son relates to the Father. He radiates God's glory now and for all eternity! Nothing can ever separate the two.

Next, the author tells us that Jesus is the exact "representation" (or image) of God. The word "representation" comes from the Greek word *charakter,* from which we get our English word "character." It's a Greek term used for the impression made by a die or stamp on a seal. Jesus is the exact representation of the substance of God. God poured every bit of who He is into the precious life He placed in Mary's womb. For nine months she carried God incarnate, and when she gave birth the exact imprint of God lived on this earth in the fleshly body of Jesus.

Finally, Jesus is the Sustainer. The King James translation says Jesus "uphold[s] all things by the word of his power." To this day, Jesus sustains everything in our universe. Without Jesus ruling and reigning over gravity, temperature, time, and space, chaos would ensue. Friend, if Jesus sustains the entire universe, how much more will He sustain us, His beloved children, when we allow Him to reign and rule over our lives? He holds us in the palm of His hand. He will sustain us until the day He ushers us into our heavenly home.

Is there anything you're trying to sustain and work in your own power? Is there chaos in your life? Prayerfully invite God into that place. Ask Him to enable you to surrender and invite His sustaining power to flood your heart and mind.

_____

_____

_____

_____

_____

More Tips

Here are a few more tips to help plant your verses deeper into your heart:

Incorporate your verse into your prayers. Talk to God about your verse in prayer. Ask Him to help you learn _and_ retain it. Pray and personalize your verse. You may have to change a few words to personalize it. For example, using this week's verse: "Father, thank You for the comfort and truth that in this hard place I know 'the Son radiates Your glory and is the exact representation of Your being, and He sustains everything by the power of His Word.' So I know You are with me and will sustain me by Your Word."

Gain context to your verse. This means read the sentences and/or passages before and after your verse. Consider why certain words or the verse itself were included. This is how we gain greater insight into what the verse means. You'll see me doing this in some of the teachings.

Read the verse in other translations or use a Bible dictionary or commentary. Using these tools helps deepen your understanding. The teachings we're doing right now are like mini-commentaries. Take notes about what you've learned in your journal or include it on your notecard for that verse.

Romans 12:10

Be devoted to one another in love. Honor one another above yourselves.

For the first eleven chapters of Romans, Paul taught some deep theology to the church. In chapter 12, Paul took a turn and explained how to put that theology into practice—how believers in Jesus should live out what we believe.

Let's add context to our verse. In Romans 12:1–2, Paul set forth "the big picture" of how God's people should live. Paul invited us to present our bodies as living sacrifices, holy and acceptable to God. He exhorted us to not conform to the world and the culture, but instead be transformed by renewing our minds with the Word of God.

When we get to our memory verse, Paul instructed us how to treat one another—more specifically, how to treat one another within the church. We are to "be devoted to one another in love. Honor one another above yourselves" (Romans 12:10).

Let's look at these two instructions. First, Paul told us how we should *feel* about one another. We're to love one another. Paul used two words for love in this verse. The first "love" is *philostorgos*, which means "the love within a family"—husband and wife, parent and child. It's described as loving, tender affection. The second "love" is *philadelphia*, which speaks more to brotherly love. In the New Testament, it's the love we have for our Christian brothers and sisters. It's the kind of love that loves deep through hurt feelings, arguments, and misunderstandings. It is love that stands up and defends another. It is also love that has compassion and empathy in another's suffering. Oh, how our divisive, angry world needs this love from God's people!

In his second instruction, Paul told us how we should *treat* one another. We're to honor one another above ourselves. Another translation says we're to "outdo one another in showing honor" (ESV). Don't just honor but honor extravagantly. By Paul's specific word choice in the Greek, he directed us to *lead the way* in honoring and loving others to the highest degree. Paul then gave practical ways to live out honoring one another in verses 11–15. Take a moment to read these verses.

Friend, we put our new nature on full display when we live out these verses. And, the best news of all, God doesn't expect us to do this in our own strength. His Spirit enables and empowers us to love and honor others, even in the most trying of circumstances. Nothing is impossible with God!

🌀 **Pray and ask God for the opportunity to put this verse into practice this week. Find a way to love and take delight in honoring another believer. Then take a moment to come back and note how God was at work in your prayer.**

Romans 15:4

For everything that was written in the past was written to teach us, so that through the endurance taught in the Scriptures and the encouragement they provide we might have hope.

I believe this is one of the most important verses in Scripture because it speaks to the role God desires His Word to play in our lives.

We find three truths in this verse:

- God sent His Word for our instruction.
- God sent His Word to provide steadfastness and encouragement.
- God sent His Word to sustain our hope.

Paul encouraged us to read God's Word. Throughout Scripture we're told to meditate on it and memorize it because it's the key to sustaining joy and hope. The Bible gives us a fresh perspective on our circumstances—God's perspective. His Word encourages us to press on, to be steadfast. That same Word, Paul said, also sustains our hope. We can fight confidently because we have the weapon of hope—hope found in the sword of the Spirit we hold firmly in our hand (Ephesians 6:17).

The stories of those who've endured hard seasons and deep loss sit in the pages of Scripture waiting to encourage and equip us to press through when everything in us wants to turn back, give up, or walk away. Friend, when we know and live the truth, it transforms our hearts and girds our minds to live grounded in abiding hope and unshakable joy, even in the midst of our unsettled souls.

⟲ **How has the time you've spent digesting God's Word, reading what was written in the past, changed your thoughts on memorizing Scripture and/or blessed you?**

_____

_____

_____

_____

_____

_____

_____

_____

Word of Encouragement

Guess what? You now have six Scriptures hidden in your heart! I'm trusting that God has done exceedingly above what you could have ever asked or imagined because of your faithfulness to persevere.

Be encouraged that this Word you're hiding in your heart every week is a _living, active, penetrating_ Word (Hebrews 4:12). It is a Word whose relevance doesn't change with the century we live in or the culture surrounding us. It is also a Word that is powerful, intended by God to effect change and transformation in our hearts and minds. When spoken in Scripture, it's a Word that convicted people of sin and converted hearts. It made the deaf to hear, the lame to walk, the blind to see, the mute to speak, and, most spectacularly, the dead to rise to life!

This is the Word you're hiding in your hearts! Are you ready for six more passages?

Galatians 5:22-23

> But the fruit of the Spirit is love, joy, peace, forbearance, kindness, goodness, faithfulness, gentleness and self-control. Against such things there is no law.

In Galatians 5, God sets forth how to live by the Spirit:

Walk by the Spirit.
Be led by the Spirit.
Bear the fruit of the Spirit.
Keep in step with the Spirit.

Thankfully, we don't do this alone. God's powerful, life-transforming Spirit flowing in and through us empowers us to walk, be led by, and bear the fruit of the Spirit.

The more we walk in step with God's Spirit and allow His Spirit to lead us, the more abundant and visible our fruit will be, the more attractive we make Jesus, and the more glory we bring to our God.

Which fruit flows most freely in you? For the fruit that doesn't, will you invite God to help you cultivate that fruit? Come back later and record how God worked through your obedience to cultivate it.

_____

_____

_____

_____

_____

Deuteronomy 31:8

> It is the LORD who goes before you. He will be with you; he will not leave you or forsake you. Do not fear or be dismayed. (ESV)

How I love the promises wrapped in this verse! Moses spoke these words to the Israelites just before God removed him as their leader and commissioned Joshua to take his place to lead them into the promised land.

Huge change was coming for the Israelites, and they didn't like it. I don't like change either. Especially when I don't know what the future holds or I'm dealing with unanswered prayers. The unknown and unanswered tend to stir up anxiety and even fear. For the Israelites, Moses's voice had become familiar and trusted because Moses spoke for God.

God knew their worries and fears, so He gave Moses the words in Deuteronomy 31:8 to comfort and encourage His people. Though spoken thousands of years ago, these living and active words still speak to us today.

God calmed the Israelites' hearts by reminding them that though Moses was leaving, He was still with them, leading them and being present in their midst. And because of those promises, they need not be afraid.

Neither should we.

Whatever storms, trials, and changes come our way, God is the same today as He was all those years ago.

Take comfort, friend. God has gone before you. He is with you, so very close, walking every step of the way. He is leading you down the path He has already paved. He loves you and has you in the palm of His hand.

How does this verse, and the promises sitting in it, comfort you today?

_____

_____

_____

_____

Psalm 4:8

> In peace I will both lie down and sleep;
> for you alone, O LORD, make me dwell in safety. (ESV)

I prayed this verse often during my unsettledness. Over time God worked through it, used it to restore my peace, and even gave me sweet rest in the midst of many sleepless nights.

King David uttered this prayer during a time when malicious people spread lies about him, undermined his authority, and questioned his leadership ability. As he always did, David turned to the Lord.

David chose *not* to be anxious and solve the battle on his own. Instead, he spoke truth to his heart about who God is. He reminded himself that he and the Israelites were God's beloved, chosen people. God heard their cries and concerns.

In the midst of his prayer, David declared two truths over his heart as he crawled into bed.

First, he would both lie down *and* sleep in peace. "In peace" means without worry and without a divided mind. Because David was God's beloved and because he was resting on God's promises, his mind could be tranquil and his heart at rest.

Second, David knew that God securely held him and watched over him even in the midst of his troubles. He was not alone. He had an unwavering trust and confidence in God's presence and sovereignty. No matter how alone he felt, God was with him and around him, protecting him and keeping him safe.

⟲ **Hem this word into your heart and declare it over your mind when unsettledness creeps in and sleep escapes you. Write a prayer and declare God's love and faithfulness over your heart. He will bring you peace and eventually sweet rest. Though it may take time, Your heavenly Father will be faithful.**

_____

_____

_____

_____

_____

2 Timothy 3:16-17

*All Scripture is God-breathed and is useful for teaching,
rebuking, correcting and training in righteousness,
so that the servant of God may be thoroughly
equipped for every good work.*

Here we find Paul teaching and mentoring Timothy, a godly young man who accompanied Paul on his missionary journeys. Paul ensured through these words that Timothy knew with all his heart that the gospel message they preached was "God-breathed."

This word in Greek is *theopneustos*, from the root words *theos* (God) and *pneustos* (breath).

Friend, let's never forget that *every* word sitting in the pages of our Bibles is God-inspired. God penetrated the hearts and minds of each writer in such powerful and pervasive ways that their words became the infallible, authoritative words of God.

Though each writer had his own style, voice, and vocabulary and wrote from his perspective, each wrote under the supernatural leading and guidance of the Holy Spirit.

In verse 17, Paul then told Timothy why God sent His Word—to prepare and equip His children for the call and purpose He has for their lives. The King James translation says God sent His Word so that the man of God may be "perfect" in his equipping. "Perfect" translates the Greek word *artios* and refers not only to the presence of all the parts necessary for completeness, but also to the further adaptation of those parts for their designed purpose.

How wonderful is that? God has given each of His beautiful and beloved children (that's you) exactly what you need to accomplish every assignment He gives you throughout your lifetime. His Word is working and relevant at every stage of your life for every purpose to which He's called and created you.

I don't know about you, but these words bring me great hope and comfort! How does this passage encourage you today?

_____

_____

_____

_____

2 Corinthians 12:9

But he said to me, "My grace is sufficient for you, for my power is made perfect in weakness." Therefore I will boast all the more gladly about my weaknesses, so that Christ's power may rest on me.

Just before Paul wrote these words, he shared a vision of being "caught up to the third heaven" that he'd seen years earlier. Paul knew in that vision he had been in the presence of God and received a word from God (2 Corinthians 12:1–5).

I can't help but wonder if God gave Paul this extraordinary vision to prepare him for the trials that lay ahead.

A few verses earlier (verse 7), Paul acknowledged that God gave him a "thorn" in his side, the "messenger of Satan," to torment him and keep him from exalting himself. As hard as those words are to accept, there's really no other way to read them. God permitted Satan to afflict Paul. The Greek word used here for torment is *kolaphizo*, which means "to strike with clenched hands." This implies repeated, recurring attacks.

Paul asked the Lord three times to remove that thorn. He didn't want it, and he told God so. This episode brings me comfort. I feel like it gives us permission to do the same.

God chose not to remove the thorn. He didn't explain why. He simply made Paul a promise.

God promised Paul that His grace would be sufficient for Paul's suffering. For Paul, that seemed enough. "Sufficient" here means to be strong enough for what Paul was battling. God's grace would be enough—it would never run dry. God also promised that His power would be made perfect in Paul's weakness.

🖎 **How do God's words and actions here make you feel like you can trust God's promises even through the really hard times?**

_____

_____

_____

Isaiah 40:31

> But those who hope in the LORD
>   will renew their strength.
> They will soar on wings like eagles;
>   they will run and not grow weary,
>   they will walk and not be faint.

Isaiah spoke these prophetic words over the nation of Judah before they entered into Babylonian captivity. This captivity was part of God's punishment for their continued disobedience and rebellion against Him.

During those years, God's people felt that He had abandoned them. Yes, He had promised that He would come and rescue them. But not until seventy years had passed! What?! Can you imagine waiting seventy years for God to fulfill His promise to you? I have trouble waiting even one day! So God's people began to question if He would ever really come.

In answer to their question, God ensured that they heard a resounding "Yes!"

How did God do this?

Isaiah reminded the Israelites in the preceding verses (verses 21–30) of God's sovereign power and mighty strength. Take a few minutes to read these verses—they will encourage you. Each verse establishes God's absolute supremacy over creation, over nations, over rulers, and, yes, even over the Israelites' captors and their captivity.

Without the preceding verses, Isaiah's words might have sounded empty, even meaningless. In reality, those verses lent divine credibility to God's promise in verse 31. This is why context is important as we study God's Word. Reading what comes before and after our verse or passage matters.

Isaiah's words prove that the God making this promise is more than able to keep it.

The good news for us is that God's promise to Israel speaks truths and principles that carry forward to us today. When we're weary, overwhelmed, anxiety-ridden, or paralyzed by fear and doubt, our God is enough. So please don't lose heart.

Let's return to our memory verse. It specifically says those who "wait" on the Lord receive the promise. That word is *qavah* in Hebrew, meaning "enduring with patience and strength." This is a waiting made easier because of *who* God is. We don't have to lose heart; we can move forward with courage because the Ruler over all the earth is with us in the wait. He is in control!

Our human strength is not enough. It's when we believe and walk in faith that our inner, Holy Spirit–empowered strength is more than enough to sustain us and enable us to soar, run, and walk.

Our God is faithful. Always. His grace is sufficient. His strength is sustaining. His power is perfected in our weakness (Deuteronomy 31:8; 2 Corinthians 12:9; Isaiah 40:31).

Will you trust God in your wait today? What first step will you take toward that trust?

_____

_____

_____

_____

_____

_____

Before we close our Scripture memory journey, I want to share one more fun tip I recently learned.

First, let's reread the sentence *before* the question I just asked you to answer:

Our God is faithful. Always. His grace is sufficient. His strength is sustaining. His power is perfected in our weakness.

Do you see what I did in that sentence? I linked together the words from our Deuteronomy 31:8, 2 Corinthians 12:9, and Isaiah 40:31 memory verses.

This idea of "linking up" of multiple passages or stories in Scripture is an ancient Jewish practice called "stringing pearls." Don't you love that custom? Stringing pearls is a teaching technique, and a brilliant one at that! Teachers string together parts of several verses or stories to bring home the major teaching point they want to get across.

As you continue to memorize verses, when time allows, remember to take them deeper by looking for common themes, truths, and promises and then string them together like precious pearls.

Okay, now let's celebrate! May I be the first to congratulate you on completing your Scripture memory journey? No matter how many verses you've memorized, it's one more than you knew when you started—and that's an accomplishment! Remember, it's not about perfect; it's about progress!

Did you ever think you could do this? I'm celebrating you and your hard work and commitment. I'm closing with one last short passage that I love. I'm using one of the tips we learned in this section.

You can choose to memorize this verse or simply enjoy the beauty of the psalmist's words about God's love and faithfulness.

Psalm 100:4-5

Enter his gates with thanksgiving
and his courts with praise;

give thanks to him and praise his name.
For the LORD is good and his love endures forever;
his faithfulness continues through all generations.

This psalm, although only five short verses, teaches a wonderful lesson. It's really the psalmist's *arrangement* of the verses that speaks volumes. Let's look at the three verses that come before our closing verses (again bringing in the context we talked about earlier).

Verse 1 invites us to praise and shout joyfully. Verse 2 invites us to worship with joyful songs of praise.

These two short verses encourage us to exalt God and worship Him with all our heart.

Verse 3, "Know that the LORD is God. It is he who made us, and we are his; we are his people, the sheep of his pasture," invites us into the knowledge of God using two of His many magnificent names. To live out verses 1 and 2, we need to *know* the One we're praising and worshiping.

The first name for God in Hebrew is *Yahweh*, the Jewish covenant name of the God of Israel. It's the personal name God gave to Moses. It's built on the Hebrew word for "I am," reminding us that God had no beginning and has no end. He simply is. He's constant and never changing.

The second name of God reveals another side of God. God is our Shepherd, and we are His precious sheep whom He knows by name. This verse gives us more knowledge in which to ground our praise.

Our verse, verse 4, "Enter his gates with thanksgiving and his courts with praise; give thanks to him and praise his name," takes us back to worship. This time we are invited into God's very presence, bringing with us thanksgiving for all He's done and for who He is. We come to adore Him and bless Him, speaking grateful, humble, surrendered words of adoration. It's about the posture of our heart—bowing low.

Verse 5, "For the LORD is good and his love endures forever; his faithfulness continues through all generations," points us back to knowledge.

Knowing God is good. He is faithful. His love is unshakable. God will never love us more (or less) than He does right now, friend. Nothing we do or don't do will change His love for us.

Our God is a God whose name and knowledge we should declare to all generations. To our children. Grandchildren. Great-grandchildren.

Let's commit today to leave this legacy of learning, knowing, praising, and declaring.

☙ **Pause here and enter into Yahweh's presence. What are you feeling, experiencing, or maybe even hearing as you sit with your Father and Creator and ponder all you've learned and accomplished as you've hidden God's Word in your heart?**

_____

_____

_____

_____

_____

_____

Thank you for saying yes to God and joining me on this leg of our solitude journey. I truly am proud of you! You've worked hard. More than that, you've brought your Father in heaven so much pleasure!

Take a few minutes to read each of the following questions and have a conversation with God. He longs to hear from you. I'm praying God will feel near and you will sense His joy and delight in your obedience and the time you've invested with Him in His Word.

☙ **What have you learned about God's Word?**

_____

_____

_____

_____

_____

◌ **What have you learned about God?**

_____

_____

_____

_____

◌ **What have you learned about yourself?**

_____

_____

_____

_____

Don't stop here, friend! I encourage you to stay committed to this holy habit. You can not only continue reviewing the verses you've memorized, but also continue to memorize new ones. Invite a friend to join you—it helps with accountability and also makes it lots more fun! You can especially exchange stories as you see God at work through your obedience. In 2021 my friend Nancy (the homemade granola girl) and I memorized forty verses! If you would have told me I would memorize forty verses in one year, I would have never believed you. Now I know it's absolutely possible because we have the mind of Christ and can do all things through Christ who strengthens us.

If you decide to continue your journey of hiding God's Word in your heart, I'm including a list of suggested verses/passages here—or you can choose your own.

James 1:5
Psalm 139:7–10
Colossians 1:15–20
Deuteronomy 6:4–9 (The Shema)
Hebrews 4:12
Proverbs 3:5–6

And remember: Don't worry about perfection. It's not about perfect; it's about progress. When you memorize God's Word, you feed your soul words directly from the mouth of God! Every word you hide in your heart is a living and active, powerful, and penetrating word. It is the bread of life . . . manna . . . bread from heaven . . . sent from Your Abba Father to bring health and healing to your body, joy to your heart, and peace to your soul.

I'm cheering you on, friend!

Now let's dive into another form of solitude: Bible study—spending time alone with God in His Word.

LORD, TEACH ME YOUR WORD

Studying—truly investing time in God's Word—transformed motherhood for me. When my daughter, Lauren, was in middle school (she's now twenty-nine), we struggled through a very difficult time. We argued nearly every day; at times our house felt like a battle zone. It was exhausting. It seemed at times she literally hated me. I felt helpless and hopeless, constantly wondering and asking, "What is wrong with her?"

One afternoon, I confronted her, unloading the anger and frustration that consumed my heart. My words were strong and harsh. At the end of my diatribe, my girl broke down in tears, something she very rarely did. Then these words poured from her lips (and really her heart):

> All you ever do is tell me what I do is wrong . . . I can't do anything right in your eyes . . . Do you realize how often you tell me I'm mean and have a hard heart? . . . Well, mom, I guess that's just who I am . . . a mean girl with a bad heart, and I will never be any different.

Her words pierced my soul. After she left the room, I fell on my knees, face to the floor, and wept—wept till I could cry no more.

My head pounding, my eyes swollen, I took out my journal and wrote these words:

> *Father, I'm struggling with my girl every single day. I'm exhausted, and I can't do this anymore. I can't deal with her. I don't know what to do. She's self-centered, angry, hormonal and lacks any semblance of kindness and compassion. She is growing up, pulling away, and it hurts so much I can't stand it. I have nothing left to give. I'm bringing her to You. I commit to fast and to pray for me, for her, and for our relationship.*

I want you to know, fasting is not a regular thing I do because I don't like how it makes me feel. I'm a bit scared of it. But it is one of the holy habits God invites us into.

I had only fasted one other time for a dear friend. We both experienced a miracle through that time of fasting and praying. Remembering God's faithfulness then, I committed to fast breakfast and lunch, one day a week, for as long as it took to hear from God.

Two weeks in, a few women approached me to teach a four-week study on wisdom for young moms. Everything in me wanted to say no. What kind of wisdom could I offer other mothers about raising their children? I felt like a complete failure in raising my own. Yet as I prayed, I felt God leading me to teach this series. In the end I accepted, and I'm thankful I did.

As I opened my Bible to study and prepare, God took me to the book of Proverbs. What I thought was a lesson for 120 women was most assuredly a lesson meant for me.

The Scriptures to which God led me (summarized next) spoke to the cry of my heart:

> The words of the godly are a life-giving fountain.
> (Proverbs 10:11 NLT)

Some people make cutting remarks,
>   but the words of the wise bring healing.
>   (Proverbs 12:18 NLT)

A wise woman builds her home,
>   but a foolish woman tears it down with her own hands.
>   (Proverbs 14:1 NLT)

A gentle answer deflects anger,
>   but harsh words make tempers flare.
>   (Proverbs 15:1 NLT)

Gentle words are a tree of life. (Proverbs 15:4 NLT)

If you listen to constructive criticism,
>   you will be at home among the wise.
>   (Proverbs 15:31 NLT)

Kind words are like honey—
>   sweet to the soul and healthy for the body.
>   (Proverbs 16:24 NLT)

These verses brought a humbling realization. This time with God wasn't about me preparing for the class I'd been invited to teach. Rather, God led me down this path to examine *my* behavior and *my* heart—not my daughter's! In fact, during my research I encountered several verses about disobedient, foolish children and not a single one caused me pause.

I passed over each one. God made it ever so clear that He had a work to do in me . . . not just my girl.

The Holy Spirit repeatedly played Lauren's words in my head—how I criticized her, labeled her, and told her that nothing she did was right. Of course, I had heard her speak these words many times in the past in a fit of anger, but I never took them to heart. I disregarded them as rude comments spewed from the mouth of an irrational, unreasonable, disrespectful teenager. This was different. This time they came through tears—her tears—her broken spirit manifesting itself.

I spoke hurtful comments to make my points, words that crushed her spirit. My beautiful, strong girl who seemed tough on the outside was broken on the inside.

I grabbed my journal. The original prayer I had written now was totally transformed:

Lord, I hear You. My heart is breaking. Please help me. Begin a work in me. I come to You in Jesus's name and surrender Lauren to You. You know what she needs right now. I don't. Teach me, Lord, how to mother her. I commit to pray about everything I've been trying to control. Teach me, remind me, and guide me every step of the way. You have created her to be different from me. She is a free spirit; I'm not. She is her own person now; help me to accept that. Help me to love who You have made her to be. Enable me to release her to You, Your protection, Your guidance, and Your counsel. Restore to me the joy of my salvation. Continue to feed me Your wisdom. Speak to my heart; show me when to speak and when to hold my tongue; put a guard at my mouth and a sentry at my lips.

Friend, if you find yourself struggling in a relationship or in circumstances you're walking through (I know I sound like a broken record here), go to God's Word. It's there, in His Word—He will speak to you and direct your steps.

And be ready, because most likely His first step will be to direct you to look within, into your own heart. Matthew 12:33–34 says:

> A tree is identified by its fruit. If a tree is good, its fruit will be good. If a tree is bad, its fruit will be bad... For whatever is in your heart determines what you say. (NLT)

Ouch! That is not what I wanted to hear. We bear fruit consistent with who and what we are. Here's the question God presented me with that day: What did my words reflect about the condition of *my* heart?

🌀 **Have you had one of these moments with the Lord, when you laid out the sins of the other person and asked God to help you help them change? How did that work for you?**

_____

_____

_____

_____

_____

Here is a simple but profound truth: **If we want more of God in our homes and our relationships, we must have more of God in our hearts.**

Period. Exclamation!

If we desire a God-honoring, Spirit-led heart, it requires examining what fills the treasury of our hearts. This takes me back to the thoughts inventory we did in an earlier chapter.

🌀 **For the next few days, inventory what fills your heart as determined by what comes out of your mouth. Do you speak words that build up or tear down? Do you spew words of impatience and anger or**

gently speak patience and kindness? Do you grumble and complain or encourage and praise?

Here's a little formula to follow:

> When we have
> God's Word **hidden** in our hearts,
> The law of God **written** on our hearts,
> His divine truths **ruling** over our hearts,
> **Good** things will flow from our hearts.
> Why? Because our treasury is full.

Proverbs 4:23 says, "Guard your heart above all else, for it is the source of life" (CSB).

◌ **Do you find yourself struggling in a relationship? Take some time before you continue reading to consider this struggle and put it into words, either in writing here or with God in prayer. Don't hold back—share exactly how you're feeling.**

◌ **How would you like to see God act or move in this relationship? Again, write your thoughts here or tell God in prayer. Be specific. Be honest with God—He can handle your honesty.**

_____

_____

_____

_____

_____

Please know your heart's cry does not go unnoticed by *El Roi*, the God who sees you. Psalm 56:8 expresses this beautifully: "You keep track of all my sorrows. You have collected all my tears in your bottle. You have recorded each one in your book" (NLT). I have always loved this verse because it reminds me that God is near. Just as He saw Mary's and Martha's tears as they mourned the loss of their brother Lazarus (John 11), He sees you. He is waiting to meet with you and is eager to do a great work in your heart and your relationships.

Let's start building a treasury of God's Word in our hearts, and when we're done we'll revisit these two questions.

STUDYING GOD'S WORD ON YOUR OWN

When I first started studying the Bible on my own, it felt overwhelming. Complicated. *Where do I begin? It was written so long ago; will I even understand what I'm reading? There's so much to learn. I'm not smart enough to read and study it on my own.* It's those thoughts that kept me attending Bible study where *other people* led me through what I was studying. For years those thoughts kept me from taking steps to study God's Word without a teacher, study guide, or agenda.

Maybe you feel the same. Those same thoughts have kept you from beginning. Or maybe you started studying and gave up because you felt like you weren't "getting" anything out of it.

◌ **How do you feel as we begin this journey of going deeper? Are you eager and excited? Intimidated? Hesitant but ready?**

_____

_____

_____

_____

After nearly twenty years of teaching Bible study, I understand.

I walked into my first Bible study nervous and overwhelmed, fearing I wouldn't fit in. Seasoned Bible study girls filled that room—women familiar with what the books of the Bible were, who wrote them, and where to find them. They knew the lingo and had the answers to the questions. I predecided before the final prayer that I wouldn't go back.

Thankfully, my friend who brought me encouraged me to not give up. I committed to go back the next week, and I'm so thankful I did because that first study led me to fall in love with God's Word in ways I could never have imagined.

My story, and the stories of other women who have experienced this same love, fuel my passion to continue teaching Bible study and writing books. I want women to fall in love with God's Word the way I did and experience in real and tangible ways how Scripture transforms hearts, lives, marriages, relationships, parenting, ministries, businesses, and even our world.

Paul's words to Timothy in 2 Timothy 3:16 provide a good dose of motivation to study the Bible: "All Scripture is breathed out by God and profitable for teaching, for reproof, for correction, and for training in righteousness" (ESV).

Paul's first few words are significant. They ensure we understand that the Bible, from beginning to end, is "breathed out by God." Every time we open the Bible, we are reading God's words. Yes, they were written by human hands, but God breathed those words into the hearts and minds of His chosen authors.

Paul longed for Timothy to understand that God filled Scripture with valuable treasures, promises, and blessings that became his as he opened God's Word. He wanted Timothy to read with great anticipation so he could know those promises and receive those blessings.

Here's what I've discovered about studying God's Word:

- It teaches us more about God, who He is, and what He wants us to know.
- It helps us see what we need to change or do differently. Though we may not like it and sometimes it won't feel good, time in Scripture reveals our sin and shows us where we need to stop, turn around, and move in a new direction.
- It teaches us how to live for Jesus and persevere in hard times, because we learn from those who have gone before us.
- And the best news of all—when we open the Bible to read, we don't do it alone. We have a teacher, the Holy Spirit, living in us, waiting to teach us and help us understand what we're reading.

We think we need a pastor, a Bible teacher, or someone we consider a "Bible expert" to understand our Bibles. But we don't. Those people are great to help spur us on in our study process but aren't necessary to personal Bible study.

God knew we would struggle to make sense of the Bible; it's why He placed His Holy Spirit in us to guide us and help us understand. First Corinthians 2:12 says, "What we have received is not the spirit of the world, but the Spirit who is from God, so that we may understand what God has freely given us." The Bible tells us that God's Spirit works in our hearts and minds to help us not only understand what we read but also how to apply it.

Let's begin with three truths about God's Word and three tips to help us study God's Word more effectively.

THREE TRUTHS: GOD'S WORD IS CONSTANT, PERSONAL, AND LIVING AND ACTIVE

God's Word Is Constant

Unlike the culture around us, God's Word never ever changes. Matthew 24:35 says, "Heaven and earth will pass away, but my words will never pass away." Peter confirmed this truth: "But the word of the Lord remains forever" (1 Peter 1:25 NLT). Joshua 21:45 says, "Not one of all the Lord's good promises to Israel failed; every one was fulfilled." Solomon echoed Joshua's declaration in 1 Kings 8:56: "Blessed be the Lord who has given rest to his people Israel, according to all that he promised. Not one word has failed of all his good promise, which he spoke by Moses his servant" (ESV). Isaiah 55:10–11 declares that God will accomplish everything His Word proclaims and will achieve the purpose for which He sent it.

David Mathis shares these words: "As much as we might suspect differently, God never goes back on his word. As he said to Jeremiah, 'I am watching over my word to perform it' (Jeremiah 1:12), even when he watches for hundreds of years. Remembering his long-term care and faithfulness may not, on its own, relieve our pain today in waiting, but through it God does provide strength to endure while we wait."[1]

God has the power to make things happen now. But He also has the wisdom and patience to watch over His Word and bring it to pass in His perfect timing, whether that's a day, a year, a generation, or a millennium.

God never goes back on His Word. Ever.

God's Word Is Personal

God sent His Word first to His Old Testament people. He spoke to Abraham, Moses, and King David and through His prophets. The Word came to them and upon them throughout their lives, allowing them to experience, know, and love Him better and more.

Then, after four hundred years of silence, God sent His Son Jesus so that His children could see, hear, and experience Him in human flesh and better understand His character and His heart. God then inspired men like Matthew, John, Peter, and Paul to put God's heart and Word in written form so that His children have access to it at any time.

One of God's psalmists said it best: "Oh how I love your law! It is my meditation all the day. Your commandment makes me wiser than my enemies, for it is ever with me. I have more understanding than all my teachers, for your testimonies are my meditation. I understand more than the aged, for I keep your precepts" (Psalm 119:97–100 ESV).

God sent His Word to speak to His people then and now. To teach us. Correct us. Train us. Reveal Himself to us. He gave us the "mind of Christ" (1 Corinthians 2:16 ESV) and His Holy Spirit (John 14:26) to receive, remember, and understand His Word. Romans 15:4 tells us that God sent His Word so that through the endurance taught in Scripture and the encouragement it provides we might have hope.

Friend, God sent His Word to make Himself known and to build our faith. To educate our minds. Protect us from false teachings. Equip us to share the truth we learn and the hope we have with others. But we can't do any of these things if we don't personally engage with God through His Word.

Only through intentional, sustained, intimate time with God in His Word will we have a personal, authentic relationship with our Creator and a deep, abiding understanding of His heart and His ways.

God's Word Is Living and Active

These two words, *living* and *active*, taken from Hebrews 4:12, mean that the Bible is relevant to our lives today. God sent it with the desire that we would interact and engage with it.

God intends to create change in our hearts and minds through these living and active words written thousands of years ago. The stories wrapped in those words transcend time. By God's Spirit living in us, those very same words and stories also carry the power to transform our hearts, homes, and relationships.

☙ Which of these truths about God's Word speaks to your heart most, and why?

_____

_____

_____

I hope these truths—God's Word is constant, personal, and living and active—encourage you.

Now I'll share some tips that help me, and I pray will help you, more confidently study God's Word.

THREE TIPS: PRAY, READ AND LEARN, AND READ AND LISTEN

Pray

Each time you open your Bible, invite God to join you. Come with a hungry heart ready to receive. Pray for wisdom and understanding. I don't always understand everything I read. I often don't see how everything fits together, and that's okay. God doesn't expect us to know everything. Invite God into your study time and ask Him to show you what He wants you to learn that day. My words of invitation come from Psalm 119:18: "Open my eyes that I may see wonderful things in your law." The key is the invitation. God will do the rest!

☙ Take a moment and write your own prayer of invitation. Make it your habit to pray your prayer each time you open your Bible.

_____

_____

_____

_____

_____

Read and Learn

After you pray, read the passage. You may need to shift your perspective a bit. Try your best not to read it like you're reading for small group Bible study or to find an answer to a specific question. Your goal is to connect with God. To understand, learn, and discover more about *who* He is. Be wide open, ready to receive what God has for *you*. It might be discovering His character. His names. His heart. His promises. His creation. The history of His people and how He related to them.

A common mistake we make when we read the Bible is immediately looking for how what we're reading applies to us personally. In reality, that should be our last step. We'll learn about this later in the chapter.

Outside resources are a great help. Later in this chapter, we'll walk through how to study a passage together. In that process, I'll share when and how to use other resources as you study. When you get to those sections, refer to the back of the book to find further help to explore what you're studying in the Recommended Resources List on pages 249-250.

Use a Study Bible

- What is a "study" Bible? The two most common types of Bibles are "study" Bibles and "life application" Bibles. Each translation will usually have a version of each.

- A life application Bible helps you better apply what you're reading to your life. It's more personal and practical.

- A study Bible enriches and deepens your faith and understanding of God's story from Genesis to Revelation. I think it's an essential tool in studying the Bible. Study Bibles include notes at the bottom of each page that provide history, background, and geographical information. They also include maps, charts, and other tools to help you navigate through and cross-reference Scripture.

Read Bible Introductions and/or Overviews

- In most Bibles, these introductions precede each book of the Bible and give a thorough overview of the book you're studying, including background content and major themes.

Read a Commentary

- Written by well-respected scholars and theologians, commentaries explain the meaning of Bible passages. They provide deeper insight, illustrations, and historical background.
- They're great resources to supplement your study time and are best used after wrestling through what you've studied on your own.
- It's important to remember commentaries are written by human authors, so they reflect the opinions and beliefs of the authors as they interpret God's Word.

Take a few minutes to open your Bible and determine whether you have a life application or a study Bible. Check out the resources the writers have provided and consider how they can guide and assist you as we continue through this lesson on studying God's Word.

_____

_____

_____

_____

_____

_____

_____

_____

_____

_____

After we pray, read, and learn, our last step is . . .

Read and Listen

I will now share a three-step process to help study a passage of Scripture. It's not a formula to follow but rather a guide to equip you to more accurately understand and interpret what you're reading.

Observe: What Does the Passage Say?

It helps to read the passage a few times. In your first reading, read to gain a first impression of the story the author's telling. Don't worry about details.

In the second or third reading, write down the details of the story. Stick to the facts. Try not to personalize, elaborate, or paraphrase. Look for who, what, when, where, how, and why. Note any contrasting or comparing words or phrases and repeated words or phrases. Determine the setting of the story. Ask questions: Where is it taking place? What is the context (what happened before and after your passage)? What is God doing? What are the people doing? If a word is unfamiliar, look the passage up in another translation or use a Bible dictionary (you can find these online).

Giving context to a verse is key and makes all the difference in progressing from knowing to learning to understanding the verse!

Be curious. Write down questions that come to mind. What challenges or confuses you? Delight in the details of what you're learning about God, His people, and His story.

Interpret: What Does the Passage Mean?

Now it's time to ask what the author is trying to communicate to his audience *at that time* because that is the audience to whom he's writing.

Do your best to avoid commentaries or study notes during this step. Wrestle with the passage alone—just you and God. Invite His Holy Spirit to speak to you as you read through the story.

If you struggle with a passage, reading it in other translations is helpful. Here's an example:

Therefore, I urge you, brothers, in view of God's mercy, to offer your bodies as living sacrifices, holy and pleasing to God—this is your spiritual act of worship. Do not conform any longer to the pattern of this world, but be transformed by the renewing of your mind. Then you will be able to test and approve what God's will is—his good, pleasing and perfect will. (Romans 12:1–2 NIV 1984)

The phrases "offer your bodies as living sacrifices" and "conform . . . to the pattern of this world" may sound a bit confusing. I've underlined these phrases in the translation that follows.

Now, let's read this Romans passage in another translation, *The Message*:

So here's what I want you to do, God helping you: <u>Take your everyday, ordinary life—your sleeping, eating, going-to-work, and walking-around life—and place it before God as an offering.</u> Embracing what God does for you is the best thing you can do for him. <u>Don't become so well-adjusted to your culture that you fit into it without even thinking.</u> Instead, fix your attention on God. You'll be changed from the inside out. Readily recognize what he wants from you, and quickly respond to it. Unlike the culture around you, always dragging you down to its level of immaturity, God brings the best out of you, develops well-formed maturity in you. (emphasis mine)

🌀 **After reading both translations, do you feel like *The Message* translation helped you understand that passage better? If so, how did it help you and how would you put what it says into practice?**

I bet you agreed that the underlined language in *The Message* gave you greater insight into what it means to offer our bodies as living sacrifices.

Another helpful tool is cross-referencing verses. Cross-referencing helps locate other verses that mention the verse you're studying or connect you with other verses on the same topic as your verse. You will find them in the margins in most Bibles. Why are they important? Because Scripture always interprets Scripture. God's Word never contradicts itself, especially on its foundational principles. The additional verses will provide more insight and understanding.

Let's try cross-referencing together. Read John 16:33: "I have said these things to you, that in me you may have peace. In the world you will have tribulation. But take heart; I have overcome the world" (ESV). In the margin of my Bible next to this verse, I find the following verses cross-referencing John 16:33: John 14:27, Romans 8:37, and 1 John 4:4. Read these verses. What insights and additional understanding do you gain from them?

_____

_____

_____

_____

_____

_____

_____

_____

_____

_____

_____

Okay, back to our study process. Once you feel like you have a grasp on the passage, summarize it in your own words, keeping in mind what you did in the first step—noting the author's words, setting, and context.

Once you summarize the passage, ask yourself these questions:

- What is the author trying to communicate to his audience at that time?
- What spiritual lesson or principle is the author trying to get across?
- Is there a tension to manage? A promise to claim? A command to obey? A rebuke or correction to pay attention to?

If you want to go deeper, desire more clarity, or want affirmation of what you've discovered in your personal study time, now is the time to bring in the outside resources I listed earlier. For example, locate and read the study notes in your Bible. Find a trusted commentary to bring in the theological and historical principles along with the truths or promises found in the passage.

Apply: What Does the Passage Mean to Me?

This is the "now what?" step in our study time. Now that we have studied the truths, promises, principles, and commands, what can we do to practically apply what we've read to our lives?

Here are some helpful questions to ask:

- What is God speaking to me?
- What are the people doing that I should be doing?
- Is this passage teaching me something new or different about God?
- Is there a command God wants me to obey, a promise He wants me to claim, a warning He wants me to heed, or a truth He wants me to know?
- What is one step I can take to move in a different direction because of the time I've spent in this passage?
- How can I respond or live differently because of what I've learned?

You may not always find a personal word or a direct action to take, and that's perfectly fine. It's just as faith-building when God gives you a grander view of Himself and His creation.

Remember, the Bible is not a textbook. It's a beautiful narrative filled with stories of living, breathing people just like you and me. God gave us His Word so that we can know Him better. Understand His heart. Receive His love. Recognize His voice. Reading the Bible this way gives us a fresh lens to lead us into a deeper understanding of God and a closer faith walk with Him.

Are you up for putting our new study process into practice?

Before we jump into our Bible study time, let's go back to where we started: my walk with my daughter and the formula the Lord gave me.

> God's Word **hidden** in our hearts,
> The law of God **written** on our hearts,
> His divine truths **ruling** over our hearts

We've spent time learning ways to put this formula into practice. When I put this into practice with my girl, it changed our relationship and our family.

My time in God's Word, and having that Word hidden in and ruling over my heart, taught me to check my words before they left my lips, asking myself questions like:

"Is this something I really need to say?"
"What is my motive in saying this?"
"Am I trying to make a point or get my way?"
"Are my words meant to hurt or heal?"
"Will my words draw us closer or push us apart?"
"Will my words draw me closer to God or farther away?"

For me the question was, what do I want to cultivate in my heart? I knew I wanted to nurture and grow my heart so that speaking words of life would become my habit and not be an exception to the rule.

For Lauren and me, God did a mighty work in our lives. Today, we have a beautiful relationship—one we treasure. It took years to come to pass and it began with me, not her.

What stunned me most is how Lauren changed. You see, she noticed the change in my heart and in my words. She saw me trying to change and even thanked me for it. And, friend, as God changed me, God changed her. Her heart softened. She became more respectful and willing to follow rules. I gave more grace. Our home was no longer a battle zone. It was a pleasant and peaceful place. On most days, anyway!

God answered my prayer exceedingly, abundantly above more than I could have ever asked or imagined. And, miracle of all miracles, I reached a point where I no longer raised my voice with my children. No yelling. Ever. It didn't even rise up within me to do it. That was a miracle. Did I speak firm words? Serious words, even discipline, yes. But it was done in such a different tone—something only God could do.

Please know, we still had (and have) arguments. Lauren still got in trouble. But it was different—not long-lasting, nor hurtful. No, it was not, and is not, perfect. As with any relationship, we are a work in progress. Through God's Word, healing and forgiveness come more quickly. We are a living testimony to the Word's power when we allow it to reign and rule over our hearts and our homes.

Okay, are you ready to do some Bible study and put into practice what we've learned?

Let's pray before we begin.

PRAYER FOR YOUR STUDY TIME

Father, thank You for this treasured time my friend will spend with You in Your Word. Help her not to be intimidated or afraid. I trust You have wonderful things to reveal to her and teach her about You and about herself. Meet with her each time she opens Your Word. She surrenders her heart and mind to You. She wants to learn from

You and about You. Hide Your truths and promises deep in her soul. Teach her. Move her. Change her. May she never be the same for the time she spends with You. I pray this in Jesus's name. May all glory, majesty, power, and authority be Yours, now and forevermore. Amen.

Okay, here we go! Remember, as you gather your Bible, your pen, and your notebook and prepare your sacred space to meet with Him, God's already there waiting to meet with you!

GENESIS 3:1–6

Now the serpent was more crafty than any of the wild animals the LORD God had made. He said to the woman, "Did God really say, 'You must not eat from any tree in the garden'?"

The woman said to the serpent, "We may eat fruit from the trees in the garden, but God did say, 'You must not eat fruit from the tree that is in the middle of the garden, and you must not touch it, or you will die.'"

"You will not certainly die," the serpent said to the woman. "For God knows that when you eat from it your eyes will be opened, and you will be like God, knowing good and evil."

When the woman saw that the fruit of the tree was good for food and pleasing to the eye, and also desirable for gaining wisdom, she took some and ate it. She also gave some to her husband, who was with her, and he ate it.

Observe: What Does the Passage Say?

List of Facts

There was a crafty serpent, made by God, present in the garden with Adam and Eve.

The serpent asked the woman if God really said they must not eat
from any tree in the garden.

The woman responded that they must not eat fruit from the tree
in the middle of the garden or touch it, or they would certainly die.

The serpent said that they would not certainly die.

The serpent told her that God gave this command because He
knew that if they ate, their eyes would be opened and they
would be like God, knowing good from evil.

The woman saw the fruit was good for food, pleasing to the eye,
and desirable for gaining wisdom.

She took some and ate it.

She gave some to her husband, who was with her.

He ate it.

The setting: near the forbidden tree in the garden of Eden

Who is present? Adam, Eve, the serpent, and God

What are the people doing? The serpent engaged Eve in a conversation. Adam is with Eve. God is not actively speaking in this passage.

Things I Noticed

God made the crafty serpent.

The serpent asked Eve a question that caused her to recall the
words God spoke to Adam about the trees in the garden.

The woman recalled God's words incorrectly.

The serpent contradicted and manipulated God's words.

Eve liked what she saw on the tree and what she heard in the
serpent's words, and she disobeyed God's instructions.

Interpret: What Does the Passage Mean?

Here I ask myself what the author wanted to communicate to his
audience *at that time* and look for lessons the author wanted the reader/
listener to learn from the passage.

God is the creator; the serpent is the created one. Therefore, God is more powerful than the serpent.

The serpent sought to cast doubt on God's Word. Jesus warned His people about the serpent's scheming in the New Testament, when he tells us Satan (the serpent) is a liar and the father of lies (John 8:44).

Eve added to God's Word, possibly revealing that when she received God's instructions about the forbidden tree (probably through Adam since in Genesis 2:15–17 when God gave the instruction it doesn't say Eve was present) she didn't listen carefully enough or didn't think it important enough to hide in her heart so it would remain (or Adam didn't communicate it effectively enough).

Eve was mistaken in even engaging with the serpent in this conversation because it opened the door for him to deceive her.

The serpent (Satan) is a deceiver. A liar.

Satan still lies to God's people today. He tempts us. He seeks to lead us away from God by sowing seeds of doubt so that we distrust God and doubt His goodness.

Satan is God's enemy and twists God's Word for his purposes.

Satan knows our weaknesses.

Spiritual warfare is real.

God's people not only need to know God's Word, but they need to hide it in their hearts so they can recall it when they need it.

Cross-Reference Verses

Genesis 3:1—Job 1:7; 2:2 (Satan roams the earth); 2 Corinthians 11:3 (just as Eve was deceived by the serpent's cunning, our minds might be led astray from our sincere devotion to Christ); Revelation 12:9 ("that ancient serpent called the devil . . . who leads the whole world astray"); Genesis 2:17 ("but you must not eat from the tree of the knowledge of good and evil, for when you eat from it you will certainly die"); John 10:10 (Satan comes to steal, kill, and destroy).

Genesis 3:2—Genesis 2:16 ("You are free to eat from any tree in the garden").

Genesis 3:3—Genesis 2:17 ("but you must not eat from the tree of the knowledge of good and evil, for when you eat from it you will certainly die").

Genesis 3:4—John 8:44 (you belong to the devil; he was a murderer from the beginning; there is no truth in him; he is a liar and the father of lies); 2 Corinthians 11:3 (just as Eve was deceived by the serpent's cunning, your minds might be led astray from your sincere devotion to Christ).

Genesis 3:5—Genesis 1:26 (mankind is to rule over the creatures that move along the ground); Genesis 3:1 (now the serpent was more crafty than any of the wild animals the Lord had made); Isaiah 14:14 ("I will ascend above the tops of the clouds; I will make myself like the Most High").

Genesis 3:6—James 1:13–15 ("God cannot be tempted by evil, nor does he tempt anyone; but each person is tempted when they are dragged away by their own evil desire and enticed"); 1 John 2:16 (For everything in the world—the cravings of sinful man, the lust of his eye, and the boasting of what he has and does—comes not from the Father but from the world); 2 Corinthians 11:3 (just as Eve was deceived by the serpent's cunning, our minds might be led astray from our sincere devotion to Christ); 1 Timothy 2:14 (the woman was deceived and became a sinner).

Sample Commentary

Here's what I learned from theologian David Guzik's commentary.

The text here does not, by itself alone, clearly identify the serpent as Satan, but the rest of the Bible makes it clear that this is Satan appearing as a serpent and invites us to read Ezekiel 28:13–19 for evidence that Satan was in Eden.

Guzik directs us to Numbers 20:8–9 and John 3:14 because the Numbers passage points to a serpent on a pole as a healing agent and Jesus identifies Himself with that serpent in John 3:14.

Satan took God's positive command (*you may freely eat of any tree in the garden, but there is only one you may not*) and rephrased it in a negative way (*you may not eat of any tree in the garden*).

Guzik also asks whether Adam effectively communicated the command to Eve. Because of this, she may not have clearly understood all that was involved, which made her more vulnerable to Satan's temptation.

He also points out how Satan effectively laid the groundwork. He drew Eve into a discussion and planted the seed of doubt about God's Word. He exposed Eve's incomplete understanding of God's Word. He then moved in for the kill, with an outright contradiction of what God said.

Guzik dissects verse 6 this way: Eve surrendered to this temptation in exactly the way John describes in 1 John 2:16. First, she gave in to the lust of the flesh (saw that it was good for food), then she gave in to the lust of the eyes (pleasant to her eyes), then she gave in to the pride of life (desirable to make her wise and more like God). Satan tempted Jesus this very same way in Matthew 4:1–11.[2]

As you consider the commentary, remember what we talked about earlier. Commentaries are written by human authors, so they reflect the opinions and beliefs of the authors as they interpret God's Word. They do not hold the same weight as God's Word.

Apply: What Does the Passage Mean to Me?

Here I ask what God is saying to me and what steps, if any, I can take to put into practice what I've learned.

This passage led me to ask: Do I truly know God's Word enough to recognize when Satan is twisting it or contradicting it?

Do I have God's Word hidden in my heart so that when Satan tempts me, or tries to deceive me, I have truth to speak back to him, like Jesus did in the wilderness (Matthew 4:1–11)?

When Satan puts thoughts in my head, do I engage him in a conversation about those thoughts, or do I immediately tune him out and turn to God and His Truth?

Do I know Satan for who he is? My enemy. The liar. The deceiver. The tempter.

Am I intentional about spending time with God in His Word as often as I can? Do I memorize it, so it's hidden in my heart and I have it on the tip of my tongue to battle back when Satan attacks?

CLOSING REFLECTIONS

I hope you've found this practical exercise helpful and equipping! I had fun writing it and going through this process with you in mind.

Here's some wisdom I've gleaned through the years: God's Word sometimes brings immediate results, immediate nourishment, and immediate relief. Those are my favorite times. At other times, God's Word works slowly. It's more like a seed sown into my heart. A seed when watered during my sacred pauses grows deeper roots to sustain and carry me when the serpent slithers near, whispering his lies and temptations. A seed when married with my prayers bears abundant fruit for my good and God's glory.

I asked you two questions near the beginning of this chapter. I've included the following questions to refresh your memory.

🖎 **Do you find yourself struggling in a relationship? Take some time before you continue reading to consider this struggle and put it into words, either in writing here or with God in prayer. Don't hold back—share exactly how you're feeling.**

⊘ **How would you like to see God act or move in this relationship? Again, write your thoughts here or tell God in prayer. Be specific. Be honest with God—He can handle your honesty.**

_____

_____

_____

_____

_____

_____

_____

Take a few minutes to look back and review your answers.

⊘ **Has what you've learned in this chapter about God's living, active, penetrating Word given you insight, strategy, wisdom, tools, and maybe even greater hope in this relationship? If so, what steps will you take to see God act or move in your heart and in this relationship?**

_____

_____

_____

_____

_____

_____

_____

_____

I encourage you to write a prayer inviting God to humbly and faithfully lead you through those steps to bring healing to your heart and to this relationship, whatever that looks like. And then commit to take one step and see what God will do. Please know I'm stopping now and asking God to show up in ways that ensure you know He's at work in your prayers and that He mightily blesses your faithful commitment and obedience.

As we close, take a few minutes and review the treasury of verses you've hidden in your heart, whether it's a few or many.

🌀 **Which verse or verses were your favorite, and why?**

_____

_____

_____

_____

_____

🌀 **How has hiding God's Word in your heart changed you?**

_____

_____

_____

_____

_____

🌀 **What are some ways God has used your time in His Word to bless your life or the life of another?**

_____

_____

_____

_____

_____

_____

Friend, I hope with all my heart this leg of our journey, taking sacred pauses to memorize and study God's Word, has encouraged you to open up your Bible more often. Hold it in your hands. Feel the pages. Read the God-breathed, living, and active words sitting in those pages. Trust by the power of the Holy Spirit that God is bringing those words alive in your heart. They are becoming part of who you are—soaking down into the marrow of your bones.

Open the Word even when you may not feel like it. Those days will come. Those hard days. Busy days. Stress-filled days. Lonely days. Just do it! Drink from the sacred well of living water. Be refreshed. Be renewed. Be refilled. Receive every last bit of what God has for you.

LORD, STILL MY SOUL

t's time to take our journey deeper. It's time to sit alone with our Creator in silence. Holy, sacred silence. No books. No music. No commentaries. No people. Just you and God.

I know this may sound uncomfortable and even scary. That's because it's not something we're used to doing. At least I wasn't. In fact, it was something I avoided for so many reasons.

As we begin, please know that God created you for this. He created you for rest. It's not the eight-hours-of-sleep kind of rest doctors prescribe, although that rest is good for you physically. Neither is it the "absence of conflict" kind of peace that the world seeks. Rather, it is a deep and abiding rest that reaches down to the depths of your soul.

The great church father Augustine said of God, "You have made us for yourself, and our heart is restless until it rests in you."[1] We find that kind of rest only when we commit to walk faithfully in the holy habits of solitude, silence, and prayer.

☙ **Take some time to reflect on the past week. How much time would you say you spent truly being silent and still? No music. No television. No podcasts. No social media. No streaming. Just being quiet—speaking no words.**

_____

_____

_____

Before we dive into this chapter, I'd like to share a story because I think when we hear testimony of something difficult or challenging, we can often see ourselves in the same challenge more easily and be encouraged. Pause for a moment and read.

MISSY'S STORY

My roles as wife, mom, daughter, friend, and high-level executive at a tech company led to a jam-packed schedule that rarely left time for restful, relaxing moments. That all changed in 2021 when several tragic events hit my life, one after the other. Any one event would have been life-altering. But all of them hit me at once. As each one hit, I cried out, "Why God? Why are you letting all this happen to me?"

The icing on the cake came with my breast cancer diagnosis, which then led to radiation treatments and a double mastectomy. I canceled everything, took leave from my job, and headed to our cabin in the mountains of Utah. I couldn't think of a better place to escape and heal from the trauma and grief, not just physically but also emotionally.

For a solid month I rested. I was still. No emails, no meetings, no Zoom calls, no trips, no conventions, no happy hours, no fundraisers. Never in my life had I taken extended time off just

---

for myself. This gave me time to engage in the holy habits God calls us to . . . solitude, silence, and prayer. I sat on my back porch, watched the birds and the deer go by and the chipmunks and the squirrels play, and listened to the gentle winds blowing through the treetops. Every morning I read my Bible and a few devotionals. I journaled a bit. I met with my therapist virtually. But mostly I communed with God and nature. I spent time praying, talking, and listening to God.

Through His Word and His people, God taught me that He really does bring good from any situation. He reminded me of how He had cared for me in the past. He manifested it in the warm and wonderful peace He so graciously laid upon my heart. I learned that I can fully trust God with the hardest and most painful parts of my story. In fact, I have already seen His promised good by how He's using my story in the lives of others as I share it. I can see and feel God's hand moving in ways that I never imagined. His constant care for me overwhelms me every day.

Rest brought peace—real, authentic, transforming peace that comes when we give our cares to God. I finally learned what it meant to completely trust God and stop trying to control every painful circumstance on my own. God knows what is best for me way better than I do, so I can relax and let go, knowing deep in my soul that He's got this and He's got me. I may not understand the reasons behind my suffering while I'm in the middle of it, but I am certain that my gracious and loving Father is working it all out for good.

Rest shifted something within me that allowed me to tune in and pay attention to what God wanted to teach me. My unsettled soul could never have received this grace-filled peace if I had not intentionally rested. Rest is now a crucial part of my self-care and soul care.

Rest only happens when we separate ourselves from all distractions so that we can be still and know God.

How do we begin? Set apart times for rest. Give your spirit a break from the busyness of life and focus on the Creator of the universe and the Creator of YOU, who loves you and wants you to grow in Him and grow closer to Him.

Don't fret or worry. Instead of worrying, pray. Let petitions and praises shape your worries into prayers, letting God know your concerns. Before you know it, a sense of God's wholeness, everything coming together for good, will come and settle you down. It's wonderful what happens when Christ displaces worry at the center of your life. (Philippians 4:6–7 MSG)

Will you join me in an activity?

Close your eyes and take four big, deep breaths from your belly. With each breath, count to four in and eight out. With each breath, think about breathing in more of the Holy Spirit and breathing out what's causing you angst and worry.

Can you relate?

Now, receive these words from your Father's heart:

Be still, my daughter.
Be still and know, my daughter.
Be still and know that I am God. (taken from Psalm 46:10)

Let's open God's Word to Psalm 46.

As I mentioned in an earlier chapter, before I study a verse or passage I like to begin with context. Context helps us determine where the Scripture fits in the book and/or chapter we're studying. It provides greater insight into the words on the page because we learn who wrote the words, who they wrote to, and why they wrote.

Scholars believe these words from Psalm 46 were written by priests (the sons of Korah) who served in the temple during or around the time when King David led and fought Israel's battles against the unbelieving nations around them.

Let's study the phrase "be still, and know that I am God" to see how these words connect with our study of silent time with the Lord.

The word "be still" in Hebrew is *raphah* (rolling "r"-a-FA) and means "to relax, release, let alone." In other words, to cease activity and be quiet.

I don't know about you, but being still is not my natural rhythm. From the time I wake up, to the time I lay my head on my pillow, I'm usually actively engaged in some activity. On the few times I've committed to quiet my heart and be still, an avalanche of thoughts come crashing in. My to-do list. Projects I need to begin. People I committed to pray for. Laundry that needs to be washed. Phone calls I need to return. And if by some miracle I do get still, I can't remain still. Within seconds, new thoughts come rushing in.

⌒ **Have you ever attempted to have a time of silence, where you don't do anything except be quiet and still your soul? If you have, what happened? How long did you make it? What interrupted it?**

_____

_____

_____

_____

_____

_____

Your Creator, the One who molded and shaped you, who knows your every need, designed you for stillness. God's Word instructs us to be still. Jesus Himself invited His disciples to stillness in Mark 6:31: "Let's go off by ourselves to a quiet place and rest awhile" (NLT). Jesus made this invitation because wherever He went, people pressed in on every side, demanding answers, seeking miracles, or expecting healing.

God does more than instruct us to "be still" in Psalm 46:10. He defines His purpose behind the command to "be still." That purpose is to "know" that He is God. That word "know" is *yada* (yuh-DA) in Hebrew. It means to cease striving, surrender, and acknowledge that God is the one and only victorious God.

There is purpose in this stillness.

It's not passive; it's active. It's a weapon we can wield to pause every other voice we hear.

Stillness is an act we engage in to gain a deeper understanding of who God is. God desires that we meditate on *who* He is. On His majesty. His holiness. His power. His sovereignty. This last word describes God's perfect control and management of the universe, this world, our families, and our lives. God continually directs all created things to follow and fulfill His divine purposes.

God is the only One who can truly refocus our hearts and minds and point us back to truth. The truth is that when life feels out of control, He is still in control.

Let's return to Psalm 46 and read the verses preceding verse 10. We discover the psalmist reminding the Israelites of *who* God is:

> God is our refuge and strength,
>   a very present help in trouble.
> Therefore we will not fear though the earth gives way,
>   though the mountains be moved into the heart of the sea,
> though its waters roar and foam,
>   though the mountains tremble at its swelling.   Selah
>
> There is a river whose streams make glad the city of God,
>   the holy habitation of the Most High.
> God is in the midst of her; she shall not be moved;
>   God will help her when morning dawns.

The nations rage, the kingdoms totter;
  he utters his voice, the earth melts.
The Lord of hosts is with us;
  the God of Jacob is our fortress.   Selah

Come, behold the works of the Lord,
  how he has brought desolations on the earth.
He makes wars cease to the end of the earth;
  he breaks the bow and shatters the spear;
  he burns the chariots with fire.
"Be still, and know that I am God.
  I will be exalted among the nations,
  I will be exalted in the earth!"
The Lord of hosts is with us;
  the God of Jacob is our fortress. (Psalm 46 ESV)

> **Read through these verses again. What words spoke most to you about who God is?**

_____

_____

_____

_____

_____

_____

For me, I cling to the words "God is our refuge and strength, a very present help in trouble" because so often in my troubles I feel alone. These names of God comfort me: Refuge. Strength. Ever-present help. Because of who God is, even when He feels absent He's not really gone. His Word tells me He's with me always, protecting and strengthening me.

"Be still" in verse 10 reminds me of the words Jesus spoke to the wind and the waves in Mark 4:39.

◌ <u>**Read Mark 4:35–41.**</u> **Who is present in this story? What happened in this passage?**

_____

_____

_____

_____

◌ <u>**Reread Mark 4:39**</u> **and write it down. What do these words mean to you today?**

_____

_____

_____

_____

Jesus rebuked the wind and said to the waves, "Quiet! Be still!" That word in Greek means "to silence, to hold one's peace." Jesus's spoken word _silenced_ and _arrested_ the winds and the waves—they both obeyed their Creator.

Friend, _this_ is the power of Jesus. Even nature obeys Him. If this is the effect Jesus's presence and words have upon the strength and power behind nature, how much more will they have on us, His beloved children!

Don't miss this truth: silence and stillness overtake us in the presence of a holy God.

Friend, this is why God commands us to be still. We need to prime our hearts so in that stillness we can step into God's nearness. We quiet our hearts, not passively but actively. When we do, we will be able to hear His voice more clearly, feel His presence more fully, and better comprehend His divinity and our humanity, His holiness and our sinfulness.

In our stillness, God will make His glory known. Our times of silence open our hearts to receive God's glory, power, work, presence, guidance, direction, and healing. Times of silence also allow space for our soul to take refuge and find strength and gladness of heart in God and His promises, even in the hard times.

In Psalm 46:8, the psalmist instructed, "Come, behold the works of the LORD" (ESV). What are the works of the Lord? His miracles and His creation, to name a couple.

Philippians 4:8 directs us: "whatever is true, whatever is noble, whatever is right, whatever is pure, whatever is lovely, whatever is admirable—if anything is excellent or praiseworthy—think about such things."

Scripture is clear.

BE STILL.

BE STILL and KNOW.

BE STILL and KNOW that I am God.

BEHOLD My works.

THINK ON what is true, noble, right, pure, lovely, admirable, excellent, and praiseworthy.

"Be still" time is a set-apart time to spend with God—to listen for and learn about Him and to praise Him and hide His Word in our hearts. More of God *in* us helps us know more *about* Him.

SCIENCE AND SILENCE

We've talked about God's instructions regarding being still and silent. Now let's look at the science and the mental benefits of being still. A 2020 study by the Cleveland Clinic listed both mental and physical benefits.[2]

Mentally, silence makes room for self-reflection and daydreaming. It opens our minds in ways that allow it to roam more freely. It activates different parts of our brain. It also cultivates mindfulness, which is maintaining a moment-by-moment awareness of what we're thinking and feeling. Mindfulness also keeps our minds open and curious to what is happening around us.

Physically, when we find ourselves in stressful situations our fight-or-flight response kicks in and activates our bodies to action. We either storm in at full speed to fight or we run as far as we can. Solitude, calm, and quiet can override fight-or-flight and tap into other areas of our nervous system.

Dr. Amy Sullivan from the Cleveland Clinic expands on this thought: "When we're frazzled, our fight-or-flight response is on overload causing a host of problems."

> We can use calm, quiet moments to tap into a different part of the nervous system that helps shut down our bodies' physical response to stress.
>
> That means, being still and silent can help you:
>
> - Lower your blood pressure.
> - Decrease your heart rate.
> - Steady your breathing.
> - Reduce muscle tension.
> - Increase focus and cognition.[3]

Yes, Lord, more of that, please!

It all comes down to our nervous system, which serves as the command center for our bodies. It originates in our brain and controls our movements, thoughts, emotions, and responses to what's going on around us. It's basically what we think, feel, and speak.

The more I studied the science behind our emotions, the more my debilitating anxiety made sense. My anxiety activated a fight-and-flight mode in my body. Months and months of that continued stress wreaked havoc on me physically and mentally.

Some stress is healthy because it enables us to adjust to new situations. It warns us of dangerous circumstances and will even send us into a fight-or-flight mode to avoid a present danger—such as when we see a child about to run into the street.

But when continued stressors assault our minds and bodies, that's when anxiety and fear tend to move in. Chronic and debilitating stress follows soon thereafter. Chronic stress can lead to symptoms like widespread aches and pains, a racing heart rate, headaches, dizziness, shaking, jaw tension, muscle pain, and digestive problems.

Because anxiety often stems from *perceived* chaos, stress also messes with us mentally. It leads to irritability, irrational thoughts, imagined fears, obsessive thoughts, panic attacks, sadness, depression, and isolation.

I experienced nearly all these symptoms at one time or another for months.

There is also a spiritual, darker side to anxiety. A dear pastor and friend to our ministry, Max Lucado, provides keen insight into this dark side in his book *Help Is Here: Finding Fresh Strength and Purpose in the Power of the Holy Spirit.*

> Satan peddles this fear. I'm convinced he runs a school dedicated to one topic: the Language of Anxiety. Somewhere in the bowels of hell, classrooms of demons are taught the dialect of dread and doubt. Were you to sit in on this class (not recommended), you would see the professor of advanced panic stalking about the room, parlaying the fine art of fear distribution. He points his bony finger in the air and speaks through a snarl. "You must sow seeds of distress in the minds of these children of God . . . Wake them up in the middle of the night. Better still, keep them awake so they cannot rest. Make sure they assume the worst. Urge them to envision a world of no escape, no solution, and no hope."[4]

We attempt to soothe and calm ourselves with external stimuli. Though this may temporarily relieve stress, anxiety, and fear, eventually those feelings return. Our temporary fixes might include alcohol, overeating, drugs, and other compulsive behavior. Or we might try to distract ourselves with our electronic devices and social media. As I mentioned earlier, my escape was bingeing old TV shows and new Netflix shows. It took my mind off myself—until it didn't. When the bingeing ended, nothing had changed. I remained in the same heightened state of stress and anxiety.

I feared being still, so I avoided it at all costs because anytime I tried, my obsessive thoughts returned—and they were relentless.

⟲ **What keeps you from being still?**

_____

_____

_____

_____

_____

_____

What I didn't understand is that if we fail to stop the fight-or-flight response, we will never have time to process our feelings and emotions. This means our bodies will continue to do what comes naturally. They react in the moment, keeping us on high alert and distracting us from sitting with our mess and dealing with it.

My darkest bout of anxiety took me down. I didn't want to leave my house. I avoided the grocery store and shopping centers because every time I went there, I felt like the aisles and walls were closing in on me. I turned down all social events, which kept me from spending time with friends, family, and coworkers. I missed parties, showers, weddings, family gatherings, and work functions. The only person I felt comfortable with was my husband and that's because he made me feel safe. But, even then, I kept to myself a lot. I couldn't sleep. Every little thing overwhelmed me—even the smallest of tasks.

I experienced chronic pain throughout my body. I didn't want to eat. I had obsessive thoughts and imagined the bad things that might be wrong with me. My uncontrolled emotions left me feeling hopeless and helpless.

I never gave my body time to refocus and recalibrate. It was in overdrive and couldn't rein itself in. My counselor warned me that my emotional distress would remain unchecked unless I took drastic action to halt it.

This is where silence and being still is key. As the Cleveland Clinic study noted, it lowers heart rate and blood pressure. It steadies breathing and releases muscle tension. It takes our eyes off our feelings and emotions and places them on something else. And, for me, that something else was God.

Psalm 46 came rushing back to me. I couldn't get the words "be still" out of my head. God, using science, the words of my counselor, and my time in the Bible, gave me hope that things could change. The three began to work in tandem in powerful ways.

I knew God was calling me to be still. It was time to stop avoiding this and making excuses.

One specific day, I decided to stop thinking about doing it and just do it.

Why that day? Because the following scene happened.

My husband and I were enjoying a few quiet moments on our back porch. I asked him, "What ya thinking about?"

"Nothing," he replied.

"No, really," I said. "I know you must be thinking about something."

Without hesitation he replied, "I'm really not."

His answer stunned me. I couldn't ever remember a time where I was thinking of nothing. He was living proof that this might be possible!

So that night I started my "be still" time by focusing on nothing but "beholding the works of the Lord"—focusing my time on what amazed me about God as Creator: the stars, planets, galaxies, oceans, His creatures, the human body, and the way a baby grows in her mama's belly.

From there I tried to silence my thoughts and empty my mind totally. This is hard, by the way! I could only do it for about five to ten seconds before my mind wandered. However, instead of giving up, I redirected my thoughts to "beholding" again. I did this night after night. Slowly but surely, I stretched my silent time (where I emptied my mind totally) to twenty seconds and then thirty seconds. When I got distracted, I returned to "beholding" and sometimes added praising God for His names and attributes.

I finally committed to trying one full minute of stillness and silence. It was hard, but each time silence came more easily. I moved from one minute to two minutes. Complete stillness and silence. No invading thoughts—pure stillness.

Something beautiful and unexpected emerged during my times of silence. God directed me to specific names of friends and family to pray for and verses to share. I truly began to hear from the Lord like never before.

On two specific occasions when I reached out to the names the Lord gave me, their responses moved me deeply. One friend and coworker received my prayer via text two days before the due date of the baby she had lost months before—a date I didn't know. The other was a dear friend whom I hadn't seen for months due to the COVID-19 stay-at-home order. I called to tell her how I missed her voice, our girls' night out, and our long conversations. I shared how much her friendship meant to me. She started crying and said that my words had come at just the right time because she felt isolated and alone.

These precious connections don't happen with every "be still" time. Sometimes I may hear nothing and spend my time continually pushing intruding thoughts out. Those are not the best days, but I don't give up. On other days the silence is sweet and intimate, enabling me to receive infillings of peace and rest. On yet other days, God calms my fears.

If you long for sweet, intimate connections with God, I invite you to join me on this next part of our journey to be still. Start small. Take baby steps.

❧ **Read Psalm 46 again slowly, inviting God to show you something new that you may not have seen or experienced the first time.**

God is our refuge and strength,
 an ever-present help in trouble.
Therefore we will not fear, though the earth give way
 and the mountains fall into the heart of the sea,
though its waters roar and foam
 and the mountains quake with their surging.

There is a river whose streams make glad the city of God,
 the holy place where the Most High dwells.
God is within her, she will not fall;
 God will help her at break of day.
Nations are in uproar, kingdoms fall;
 he lifts his voice, the earth melts.

The Lord Almighty is with us;
 the God of Jacob is our fortress.

Come and see what the Lord has done,
 the desolations he has brought on the earth.
He makes wars cease
 to the ends of the earth.
He breaks the bow and shatters the spear;
 he burns the shields with fire.
He says, "Be still, and know that I am God;
 I will be exalted among the nations,
 I will be exalted in the earth."

The Lord Almighty is with us;
 the God of Jacob is our fortress.

◌ **Now take some time to ponder these questions.**

- **What does the son of Korah (the author of this psalm) tell you about God?**

_____

_____

_____

_____

- **What did he instruct the people to whom he was writing to do?**

_____

_____

_____

_____

- **What is God speaking to you today?**

_____

_____

_____

_____

Remember my confession about my "be still" time? I didn't start well. Each time I started, I failed. So I changed my strategy.

Step One: Invite God In

First, I began my "be still" time inviting God through a simple prayer to meet me in it.

And guess what? I didn't even try the silent part! Instead, I focused on the "being still" and "knowing God" part by "beholding" His works, as it says in Psalm 46:8. The best way to find "content" for your "beholding" time is to search your Bible for images and descriptions of God and His creation. Here are a few places to begin: Psalms 8, 19, 139, 145, 147, and Job 38–41.

Step Two: Start Small

Commit to ten to fifteen seconds of silence, trying your best to set your mind on nothing. Focusing on your breathing is a great way to begin. I like to think about breathing in more of the Holy Spirit and breathing out what's causing my anxious or fearful thoughts. And if silence feels impossible, like it did for me at first, turn your mind from silence to "beholding the works of the Lord," picturing and thinking on the beauty of God's creation. Do this for a few days or maybe a week. Remember, you're retraining your brain to do something it's not used to doing, so it will take time. Be patient.

Next, do your best to increase it to thirty seconds. When thoughts press in, redirect to breathing and beholding or meditating on the names of God (we'll get to that in a bit) or to praising God using His attributes (that's coming too!).

℘ **Try this for one or two weeks, several times a week. Make it your goal to reach one minute with God in silence and quiet. Move to "beholding the works of the Lord" when distractions come your way. Journal your progress—what you feel, what you hear, and what you physically experience.**

_____

_____

_____

_____

_____

_____

_____

_____

_____

Step Three: Add One Minute of Stillness and Silence

Keep working on your one minute of stillness and silence and then try to extend it one more minute. It's hard—don't give up. When thoughts of anything other than God intrude, push them away with what we've talked about. You can praise God for who He is—His goodness, faithfulness, love, wisdom, patience, fruit of the Spirit, and majesty. If you love worship, meditate on the lyrics to familiar hymns and worship songs.

Remember, there aren't rules here—only guidelines. There's no deadline. This isn't a test or an assignment. This time is a gift—it's just God and you. Make an intentional decision to not get stressed or mad. And, most of all, don't give up.

Honestly, about the second week in, for about fifteen to twenty seconds I truly thought of nothing. My mind was blank, and it felt so foreign. But it also felt good and peaceful. And when thoughts crashed in, I immediately turned them to praise or praying the names of God or beholding God's works.

Step Four: Add Another Minute or Two of Silence

Use this added time to invite God to take you deeper and minister and speak to you in your stillness or reveal His presence and power in new ways as you seek to "know that He is God."

More than anything, *listen* in the stillness and the silence—really listen. This will be hard because those distracting thoughts may come flooding in. I shared earlier how during my "be still" times God laid specific names on my heart to pray for and specific ways to follow up on my prayers, such as to send a text or make a call. It was incredible how simply being still freed my heart and mind to be available to the Lord in ways I hadn't experienced before. It made space for me to truly listen.

What God did in those minutes opened the door for me to be the voice of Jesus for a friend who needed it, so that I could minister to a woman in her loneliness. What a precious privilege, to be used by God to draw those we love closer to Him and help them feel seen and heard!

And most amazing to me is the posture in which I now begin my days. It's different. I start my day from a more centered, peaceful place. It's hard to put words to the feeling. But it's different—and it's full and sweet.

Step Five: Remember That Being Still Is a Gift That Keeps on Giving

Sometimes God will do exceedingly more than we imagine. And that happened for me a few months after I began my times of stillness and silence. In fact, what I'm about to share has been some of the best fruit God produced during my "be still" time. It's when God laid on my heart to memorize Scripture (which we talked about earlier). A few months into memorizing, I loved it so much and saw God actively at work in it that I invited my social media friends to join me. That journey led to the writing of this book. And that journey led to this invitation for *you* to join me.

Today, I stand amazed at how God has multiplied the fruit produced from one woman's commitment to solitude, silence, and prayer!

Now I pray the same for you as you commit to your times of solitude, silence, and prayer. May God show up in creative, amazing, Spirit-filled, Spirit-led ways that draw you closer to His heart and His Word.

Step Six: Journal What You Experience (It Increases Seeing God's Handiwork)

At some point in time, I decided to record the times God met me in specific ways in my "be still" time. I recorded it in a journal my aunt gave me.

My journal has four very short sections: Worries, Praise, Prayers, and Promises of God. They all fit on one page. I write my worries and my praises first. Whenever I see God at work through a verse I've shared or a prayer I've sent, I record it under the Praise section. I record the thoughts, names, fears, and worries God brings to mind in my Worries and/or Prayer sections. I record prayer requests shared with me in the Prayers section.

In the Promises of God section, I often write my memory verse for the week. Often by the last day of the week, I'm close to knowing it by heart. When time allows, I also recite the earlier verses. True confession here: I may need to peek back for refreshment sometimes. But with each week, God solidifies the verses in my heart more and more.

It amazes me how creative "be still" time can be!

I have a dear friend, Nancy, who has joined me on this memorization journey. We meet periodically to go over our verses and share what God has done. In fact, the last time we met she had memorized Colossians 1:15–20. What amazed me was how she recited the thirty-two verses we had memorized *and* that long Colossians passage. I had not even tackled memorizing passages that had more than two or three verses. Now I'm memorizing this Colossians 1 passage. I'm stunned by how quickly the Lord is hiding it in my heart.

You see, my friend, we don't memorize alone. We have the Holy Spirit living in us to teach and remind us of God's Word. He's delighted that we're memorizing His Word and rewards our efforts!

BEING STILL IS ALSO ONE OF OUR GREATEST WEAPONS

"Be still" time is one of the greatest weapons we have in our mental battles. Whether it's fear, anxiety, unforgiveness, bitterness, doubt, or addiction, mental battles are fought in our flesh (our human emotions and feelings), most specifically in our minds. Our flesh fights what we know the Spirit is leading us to do. Being still enables us to step outside our mental battle and fix our eyes on the one and only One who can rescue, redirect, and renew our hearts and minds.

Our times of solitude and silence make room for the Spirit to move and ensure that the living, active, penetrating Word in us does the work God created it to do. They pave the way for God to fill us with *His* strength, presence, and power to move us forward with hope and confidence on our journey.

Remember, there are no hard and fast rules in "be still" time! It's just you and your Father in heaven intimately connecting in the sweet stillness of time.

Trust me—only the very best fruit can come from sitting at the feet of the One who knit you together in your mama's womb. He formed and shaped you. He loves you more than anyone else in the universe. He knows the plans He has for you and is waiting to fulfill each one.

I pray that as you lay your head on your pillow tonight, you hear these words from your Abba Father: *"My beloved daughter, be still. Be still and know. Be still and know that I am God. Come and meet with me. I'm waiting."*

PRAISING GOD THROUGH HIS NAMES

Sometimes it's hard to know how to spend silent time. One of my favorite ways to engage with God during this time is praising Him through His many names.

I was years into my walk with the Lord before I knew God had names other than "God" and "Father," let alone hundreds of names. Now, years later, one of my favorite ways to spend my "be still" time is pondering and praising God through His many magnificent names. In fact, I love studying God's names so much that I wrote a book on the names of God, *I Know His Name: Discovering Power in the Names of God.*

How do you praise God using His names? As we talked about earlier, silence is hard. Our minds easily wander, so praising God through His names is another way to redirect your thoughts. It helps keep your eyes fixed on God, not on yourself. It also takes you even deeper into that sacred space as you seek to soothe your unsettled soul.

A Bit of History on God's Names

Have you ever noticed how many names God has in the Bible? If you haven't, you're not alone. As I said earlier, I didn't know God had other names until my friend Lisa Allen taught me that God not only has many names but each of those names has a purpose. Sometimes it points to a specific attribute of God or His character or how He relates to His people. When I asked her how God came to have these names, she explained that sometimes God gave Himself the name. What fascinated me most was when Lisa said God's people sometimes gave Him a name that reflected what happened during their divine appointment with Him.

Biblical history reveals that names often carried great significance. Yes, a person's name helped distinguish one person from another, as names still do today. But they also meant much more.

Sometimes a name signified a person's origin. The opening story of Genesis provides a great example. First, God created and named Adam. God then created the first woman and gave Adam the honor of naming her, and he named her Eve. Let's read the words Adam spoke when he named her in Genesis 3:20: "Adam named his wife Eve, because she would become the mother of all the living." Her name in Hebrew means "living." Eve had the honor and privilege of being the first human to bring human life into God's creation. She holds the title of earth's first mom.

Sometimes a name signified a person's purpose. For instance, God often changed people's names when He sent them in a new direction and/or placed a new call on their lives. We see this when Jesus called one of His first disciples, a fisherman named Simon, to follow Him. John 1:42 tells us that Jesus changed Simon's name: "Jesus looked at him and said, 'You are Simon the son of John. You shall be called Cephas' (which means Peter)" (ESV). That name "Cephas" is "stone" in Greek. At the time Jesus gave Simon his new name, his character didn't seem to reflect that name. But after Jesus's death and resurrection, Peter became the stone—the rock—for which he was named. He was the rock upon which God built the New Testament church.

Names also signified a person's characteristics or circumstances. Abraham and Sarah (both over ninety years old) laughed when God told them that Sarah would give birth to a son. When she did give birth, they named the child Isaac, which means "laughter" (Genesis 21:6). Isaac grew up and had twin sons with Rebekah. They named the oldest twin Esau, which means "hairy" because of how much hair he had at birth (Genesis 25:25).

Today, names still hold significance. My son's name carries history with it—his name is Edward Montague Blight IV. We call him Bo. I know, how do you get Bo from that name? That's a story for another time. His name carries with it a legacy and a history. It represents his father, his grandfather, and his great-grandfather, and will hopefully always remind Bo of who he is and guide him as he makes decisions throughout his life.

Throughout Scripture, God's names also carry significance. For every need, God provides a name that meets that need. The more we learn and study His names, the better we understand God's nature, personality, and character as well as His grandeur and goodness.

Let's travel to the book of Matthew to see what Jesus has to say about God's name. In Matthew 6, the disciples asked Jesus how they should pray. Jesus answered with what we call "The Lord's Prayer." Though it feels like a rote prayer, I consider it a recipe for prayer. It is a model Jesus gave to guide His followers (and us) as they sought to deepen their prayer life.

The opening words of this prayer signify the honor to be given God's name. After opening the prayer with God's name, "Father," Jesus prayed, "hallowed be your name" (Matthew 6:9). When we "hallow" something, we treat it as holy and sacred. We set it apart as something worthy of our absolute devotion. So when we hallow the name of God we regard Him with complete devotion and loving admiration.

Friend, since God's names are the key to knowing God more deeply and understanding Him more fully, we're going to explore many of these names to help us move from simply knowing *about* God to truly *knowing* Him.

Let's pray before we begin:

Heavenly Father, show Yourself to me. Reveal Your many magnificent names. Teach me each one so I can know You better and understand You more fully. I know when I do this, Lord, I will know myself better because I am Your child, created in Your image. I pray this in Jesus's name, amen.

Before we reflect on God's names, let's do a quick theology lesson on a word we'll see often as we begin learning God's names. The word is *"el."* This Hebrew word is a generic word for "god," and can refer to any god. But when we see *"El"* in the Bible, it's capitalized and is the first word preceding many of God's names. The words following *"El"* reveal a character trait or attribute that distinguishes the God of Israel from all other gods.

For example, in God's name *Elohim* the writers added *"im"* to the end of the word beginning with *"El,"* which is like adding an "s" to an English word and making it plural. Why is this important? Because although *Elohim* is plural, the Bible uses it exclusively with a singular verb.

We'll learn more about why this is significant when we study *Elohim*, God our Creator.

Now my favorite part! Let's begin our adventure into God's magnificent names. With each name, I'll share both the first place we find it in the Bible and the story behind the name. I love to learn God's names this way because it brings deeper meaning and intimacy to each name as we meditate on it and pray it.

Jehovah/Yahweh

*pronounced jah-hoe-vah/yaw-way

We'll begin with God's most sacred name, *Yahweh*. It is the intimate name God revealed to the Israelites to remind them of His greatness and emphasize that they were His possession and inheritance. It is a name so sacred that none of the Israelites, the priests, or even the scribes would speak it out loud.

Yahweh comes from four Hebrew consonants, YHWH. Scribes later inserted the vowels to form the word *"Yahweh."* Some Bible translations use the word *"Jehovah."*

God first introduced this name in Exodus 3:15 when Moses asked Him who he should say was sending him to lead the Israelites. God's response goes to the essence of who He is: "Say to the Israelites, 'The LORD, the God of your fathers—the God of Abraham, the God of Isaac and the God of Jacob—has sent me to you.' This is my name forever, the name you shall call me from generation to generation."

To make His intent abundantly clear, God preceded this announcement with two other power-packed statements: "I AM WHO I AM" and "This is what you are to say to the Israelites: 'I AM has sent me to you'" (Exodus 3:14).

In verse 14 God connected His name, newly announced in verse 15, to the Hebrew verb "I Am," meaning "The One Who Is." *Yahweh* is the Self-Existent One. With this name, God communicated that He is not a created being. He alone is the Creator. *Yahweh* had no beginning and has no end. This is a name unique to God and sets Him apart as the One True God amid all the gods worshiped in the culture in which the Israelites lived.

Our Bibles don't use the name *Yahweh*. The English language does not have an exact translation for *Yahweh*, so our translations use the word "LORD" in all caps. When you see "LORD" in all caps or all small caps in the Old Testament, you know the writer is referring to *Yahweh*. When you see "Lord" (not all caps), the author is usually referring to God's name *Adonai*, which emphasizes God's lordship.

As you study God's names, you'll find many of them coupled with the name *Jehovah/Yahweh*. The word following *Yahweh* reveals a specific attribute of God.

⊙ **As you ponder Yahweh in your times of silence, reflect on this name's meaning. Yahweh is not a distant God who created earth and left us alone to figure life out on our own. He is near. He is I Am. He was. He is. He will always be. In your most lonely and trying times, I pray this name reminds you that you are not alone. Consider what this name means personally as you consider your past, present, and future.**

Elohim: God Our Creator

pronounced el-low-heem

God opens Genesis 1:1 with the name *Elohim* to ensure that we know *who* created the heavens and the earth. In our Bible we see the word "God," but in the original Hebrew it's *Elohim*.

I introduced this name earlier and shared how the noun *Elohim* is plural but used exclusively with a singular verb. Why does that matter? Because *Elohim* differs from the pagan gods worshiped by the unbelieving nations surrounding the Israelites. It's a name unique to the Bible. *Elohim* captures the doctrine of the Trinity. Three persons in one God—God the Father, God the Son, and God the Holy Spirit. Singular yet plural.

Though the exact meaning of *Elohim* is unknown, this name incorporates strength and power and speaks of God's supremacy as He reveals Himself through creation.

"In the beginning God created" (Genesis 1:1). Friend, our universe is not an accident. God, the master architect, carefully designed and crafted each stage of creation's design. *Elohim*'s invisible qualities echo throughout our world in every natural wonder, every majestic mountain, and every roaring sea. The daily rising and setting of the sun and stars happen at His command.

And—the best news of all!—we, His daughters, were Elohim's final and crowning act of His creation. *Elohim* created us in His image. I think He saved the best for last, don't you agree?

☙ As you ponder *Elohim* during your sacred silent time, remember that a living, personal, creative *Elohim* crafted the beauty that lies before and around you. But, even more precious, also remember that *Elohim* shaped and patterned you to be like Him. To reflect His likeness, His heart, and His mind. What does it mean to you that you carry the DNA of your Creator?

El Elyon: The Most High God

*pronounced el el-yon

We first find *El Elyon* in Genesis 14:18. A mysterious, ancient king and priest gave God this name during his encounter with Abram (Abraham's name before God changed it). His name was Melchizedek—I'll call him "King Mel." At one point during their encounter, King Mel presented Abram with bread and wine and blessed him with these words, ". . . Blessed be Abram by God Most High, Creator of heaven and earth. And praise be to God Most High, who delivered your enemies into your hand" (Genesis 14:19–20).

We learned earlier that *El* means "God." King Mel connected *El* with *Elyon*, which means "highest, uppermost." With this name, the ancient king and priest ensured that Abram knew Israel's God, our God, is supreme above all other gods. He sits in the highest place of honor in the heavens.

Another one of my favorite places where we see *El Elyon* is when David sang a beautiful song of praise to God after He delivered him from the hands of King Saul (2 Samuel 22). Take a few moments to read the entire chapter. I'm including a few passages to give you a taste of its beauty:

> The Lord is my rock, my fortress and my deliverer;
> my God is my rock, in whom I take refuge,
> my shield and the horn of my salvation.
> He is my stronghold, my refuge and my savior—
> from violent people you save me . . .
>
> In my distress I called to the Lord;
> I called out to my God.
> From his temple he heard my voice;
> my cry came to his ears . . .
> Out of the brightness of his presence
> bolts of lightning blazed forth.

The Lord thundered from heaven,
  the voice of the Most High resounded.
He shot his arrows and scattered the enemy,
  with great bolts of lightning he routed them.
  (vv. 2–3, 7, 13–15, emphasis mine)

🔊 As you ponder *El Elyon* in your silent time, remember that He reigns over and above everything in the heavens, on the earth, and under the earth. How does this name encourage you as you wrestle with worries or circumstances that hold you captive? How can knowing that God is ruling and reigning over your life change your perspective?

El Shaddai: Lord God Almighty

*pronounced el-sha-die

God revealed Himself as *El Shaddai* in Genesis 17:1–2. He chose this name when He announced the everlasting covenant that He would establish with Abram and his descendants. "When Abram was ninety-nine years old, the Lord appeared to him and said, 'I am God Almighty; walk before me faithfully and be blameless. Then I will make my covenant between me and you and will greatly increase your numbers.'"

How precious this name must have been for Abram in his day and time, surrounded by idol worshipers who revered gods made of wood and stone! He understood the significance of those Hebrew words—God was telling Abram that *He* was "God Almighty." *He* was all-powerful. *He* was the One True God.

Don't you love that in our language, the two words joined together that make up the word "almighty" are "all" and "might"? Friend, this word points to the truth that God's power is unlimited and all-encompassing. Nothing is outside its scope. Nothing is impossible with *El Shaddai.*

God timed this name intentionally. He shared the name *El Shaddai* to childless Abraham and Sarah just *before* he told them, at nearly one hundred (Abraham) and ninety (Sarah) years old, that they would have a son (Genesis 18:10). *El Shaddai's* promise sounded so outrageous that Sarah laughed when God told them (Genesis 18:12). However, with *El Elyon's* name in mind Abraham could trust that God was fully able to fulfill this miraculous promise to give them a son and descendants too numerous to count that would make him the father of many nations.

☙ **As you ponder *El Shaddai* during your times of silence, remember that your God is a God of the impossible. He resurrects life from death, brings hope from despair, peace from anxiety, and love from hate. He can do exceedingly abundantly above what you can ask or imagine when you simply call on His name, *El Shaddai.* Where do you, or someone you love and care about, need to know *El Shaddai* more intimately today?**

Abba: Father

*pronounced ah-bah

We don't meet God as *Abba* until the New Testament. *Abba* is an Aramaic word. It parallels the Hebrew word *av,* from where *abba,* or "father," is derived.[5] We only find the term *abba* three times in the New Testament—in Mark 14:36, Romans 8:15, and Galatians 4:6—spoken by Jesus and Paul. We first find Jesus using *Abba* when He cried out to God in the garden of Gethsemane. Of all God's many magnificent names, in Jesus's darkest hour, in His deepest suffering, He called upon the most intimate and personal name, *Abba, Father* (Mark 14:36).

We see *Abba, Father* again in Romans 8:15–16: "Instead, you received God's Spirit when he adopted you as his own children. Now we call him, 'Abba, Father.' For his Spirit joins with our spirit to affirm that we are God's children" (NLT). Paul here reminded us that when we accept Jesus as our Lord and Savior, God adopts us into His family and we become His beloved child.

Young Jewish children called their fathers "Abba" during Jesus's time. It's kind of how we use "Daddy" or "Papa" today. *Abba* is a relational name, conveying familiarity and closeness. By using this name, *Abba* ensures that we know He desires a personal relationship with us. We can feel comfortable sharing our deepest thoughts, dreams, fears, worries, and struggles with Him.

Some of us may not have good earthly fathers. They've hurt us, disappointed us, and maybe even abandoned us. Thankfully, our *Abba Father* is different. His love is pure. His heart is good. Always.

Your *Abba Father* loves you with a lavish love (1 John 3:1). *Abba* adopted you into His family and calls you His child (John 1:12–13; 2 Corinthians 6:18). *Abba* is always near (Psalm 34:18). *Abba* will never leave you nor forsake you (Deuteronomy 31:8).

☙ **As you ponder your *Abba Father* in your sacred silent time, remember that Elohim, the God who created the world, created you. He calls you His daughter. Nothing will ever change that or separate you from Him. He loves you with a perfect love. Read the verses I just referenced. How do they encourage you? Will you allow *Abba* to take you in His arms so you may receive His love and protection today?**

Jehovah Shalom: The Lord Is Peace

*pronounced shah-lome

In the Old Testament book of Judges, God appeared in the form of an angel and spoke to a man named Gideon. During that encounter, God called Gideon to lead the Israelites into battle against one of their most hated enemies. Gideon hesitated, explaining how completely unqualified he was for God's huge assignment. But God didn't give up. He gave Gideon a sign and spoke these words: "Peace! Do not be afraid. You are not going to die" (Judges 6:23).

We find our next name of God in this holy moment. Judges 6:24 says, "So Gideon built an altar to the LORD there and called it The LORD Is Peace." This name in Hebrew is *Jehovah Shalom.* Shalom means "completeness, soundness, welfare, peace." It's more than an absence of conflict or inner calm. It's a deep and abiding peace that passes all understanding, beyond what our world could ever give.

When Gideon understood the depth of the meaning of this name, and the promises standing behind it, he gained the confidence he needed to lead the Israelite soldiers into battle. He fully trusted that *Jehovah Shalom* was walking with him. I pray this instills the very same confidence in you.

☙ **As you ponder *Jehovah Shalom* in your silence, remember that you can't muster up peace. You can't create peace. Rather, you receive it from the One who is peace. So keep your eyes fixed on *Jehovah Shalom* and not on your circumstances. When you do, you'll find the same precious promises that Gideon did. You will find peace. And in that peace you will find rest. You will find courage. You will find hope. How will you take hold of and walk in the fullness of *Jehovah Shalom*'s peace today?**

Jehovah Rapha: The Lord Who Heals

*pronounced *ra-fee*

God revealed His name *Jehovah Rapha* to the Israelites three days after He parted the Red Sea. The Israelites had gone without water during those three days, and when they finally found water it was bitter. They did as they often did: they grumbled and complained to Moses. Moses prayed for God to extend grace to His people. God answered Moses's prayer, as He always did, and the Lord transformed the bitter water into sweet water.

After this miracle, the Lord revealed a new name: "He said, 'If you listen carefully to the Lord your God and do what is right in his eyes, if you pay attention to his commands and keep all his decrees, I will not bring on you any of the diseases I brought on the Egyptians, for I am the Lord, who heals you'" (Exodus 15:26).

Jehovah Rapha means "The Lord who heals" in Hebrew.

Rapha means "to heal, to restore, to make whole." The incomprehensible truth is that God's healing is so broad and wide that it invades beyond the physical into the spiritual, emotional, and eternal spheres. God's healing grace—His healing strength—is sufficient and is made perfect in our weakness. In our grief. In our brokenness. In our disappointments. In our loss. In our pain. In our nation. In our world.

☙ **As you ponder God in your sacred silent time, remember that *Jehovah Rapha* is your Healer. He's waiting to pour His sweet, living, healing water into the diseased, hurting, broken, grieving spaces of your soul and bring you healing and wholeness. Where do you (or someone you love) need *Jehovah Rapha* today? Write a prayer to Him inviting Him to overwhelm and bless you with His healing power.**

Jehovah Yireh: The Lord Will Provide

*pronounced *ji-ruh*

God gave Abraham this name on Mount Moriah the day He asked him to sacrifice his son, Isaac. Back in Genesis 17, God promised Abraham that he would be the "father of many nations" (Genesis 17:5). God gave Abraham his son, Isaac, to fulfill that promise. Now God was asking Abraham to sacrifice Isaac. Was He contradicting His promise?

Yet, despite the facts that lay before him, and what he saw with his physical eyes, Abraham chose obedience. He trusted God's promise and believed He would provide another offering.

Abraham obediently built an altar, though he saw no provision other than his son. He then bound his son and laid him on the altar, though he still saw no provision. He then took the knife and stretched out his hand to sacrifice his son, still seeing no provision.

At the very last moment, just before Abraham drew back the knife to slay Isaac, an angel of the Lord called to him from heaven, "Abraham! Abraham! . . . Do not lay a hand on the boy . . . Do not do anything to him. Now I know that you fear God, because you have not withheld from me your son, your only son" (Genesis 22:11–12). Provision finally came: "Abraham looked up and there in a thicket he saw a ram caught by its horns. He went over and took the ram and sacrificed it as a burnt offering instead of his son" (Genesis 22:13). This was God's perfect provision.

We find our next name of God here: "So Abraham called that place The LORD Will Provide. And to this day it is said, 'On the mountain of the LORD it will be provided'" (Genesis 22:14).

Don't miss the significance of this story, friend. Abraham's obedience led to *Jehovah Jireh's* provision.

How could Abraham have obeyed so completely, knowing the incredible cost of *Jehovah Jireh's* command? Hebrews 11 gives us great insight: "Abraham reasoned that God could even raise the dead, and so in a manner of speaking he did receive Isaac back from death" (Hebrews 11:19).

And marvel with me as we consider this next thought. The first time we see *Jehovah Jireh* is when a father (Abraham) willingly offered up his son. Sound familiar? God did the very same for us. When sin separated us from *Jehovah Jireh*, Jesus laid down His life, willingly taking our sin upon Himself. Jesus is *Jehovah Jireh*'s ultimate provision.

      Are you in need of provision? As you ponder *Jehovah Jireh* in your times of silence, remember that His provision will come when you lay down your Isaac and trust Him. *Jehovah Jireh* stands ready to provide. He owns the cattle on a thousand hills (Psalm 50:10). His resources are unlimited. His love is unconditional. His hope is everlasting. Take time now to lay down your Isaac. Give it to *Jehovah Jireh* and patiently, with anticipation, watch and wait for His provision.

Jehovah Raah: The Lord Is My Shepherd

*pronounced *ro-hah*

King David made this name of God famous in Psalm 23:1: "The LORD is my shepherd, I lack nothing." But we find it earlier in God's Word when one of the great fathers of the faith, Jacob, called God "my shepherd" in Genesis 48:15. Jesus carried this name forward to the New Testament in John 10:14: "I am the good shepherd; I know my sheep and my sheep know me."

The name *rohi* derives from the root word *ra'ah*, which means "to pasture, tend to, or graze." A shepherd is one who feeds or leads his flock to pasture.

David probably understood and treasured the true meaning of this name of God because he grew up shepherding his father's sheep. He fed and led them. He tended and cared for them. He pursued those who wandered away and brought them back to the sheepfold. He protected and defended them against wild animals.

David gave us great promises about *Jehovah Raah*, our Shepherd. He brings us contentment. In Him we lack nothing. He gives us the confidence to lie down and sleep in peace. He feeds us His living and active Word and quenches our thirst with His living water.

Our Shepherd comforts our broken hearts. He refreshes our weariness. He rescues us from fear, anxiety, and despair. He finds us when we are lost or in the middle of a big old mess.

Our Shepherd guides us on good paths. He gives direction when we don't know which way to go, always leading us back to safety and security in His arms. And even when we find ourselves on the darkest paths where we don't see or feel God, our Shepherd is with us, leading the way and providing for our every need.

Our Shepherd comforts and protects us with His rod and His staff. His rod, though it can feel uncomfortable and even painful, is meant for our good. It corrects and redirects us back to His good plans and purposes. A shepherd's staff is his walking stick, his support. And our Shepherd is our staff. He walks alongside us to support and comfort us.

𝕆꙳ **As you ponder this name of God in your silence, remember that just as a shepherd provides everything his sheep need, *Jehovah Raah* walks alongside you. You no longer have to wrestle through the hard things alone. He is with you on your very best of days and on your very worst of days. His heart has only the very best in mind for you. He proved this when He, the Lamb of God, laid down His life for you. What does it mean to know Jesus as your Shepherd? Take time to thank Him for the gift of His presence and provision as your Shepherd.**

El Roi: The God Who Sees

*pronounced *row-ee*

An Egyptian servant girl named Hagar gave this name to God in Genesis 16. How did this come about? Since Abram's wife, Sarai, couldn't conceive, she schemed a plan for Abram to sleep with Hagar (her servant girl), reasoning that Hagar would give them the child God had not. After Hagar became pregnant, Sarai mistreated her terribly. To escape Sarai's cruelty, Hagar fled to the desert.

Scripture tells us that God found Hagar: "The angel of the LORD found Hagar near a spring in the desert . . . And he said, "Hagar, slave of Sarai, where have you come from, and where are you going?" (Genesis 16:7–8). Scholars believe this is the first of many appearances of Jesus coming to earth before He came as a baby in the New Testament. Think about what this means! Jesus, the Son of God, left heaven and cloaked Himself in a temporary body to minister to Hagar. And did you notice? He called her *by name.*

God instructed Hagar to go back to Abram and Sarai and submit to Sarai. How hard that must have been! But He also gave her a promise: He promised Hagar that she would give birth to a son and through him He would increase her descendants so much that they would be too numerous to count.

Hagar commemorated God's intervention and rescue of her with these words: "So she called the name of the LORD who spoke to her, 'You are a God of seeing,' for she said, 'Truly here I have seen him who looks after me'" (Genesis 16:13 ESV).

Hagar expressed her gratitude by giving God a special name: *El Roi. Roi* in Hebrew means "looking, seeing, sight." Hagar's words are beautiful: "I have now seen the One who sees me." She heard God. She saw God. And, best of all, God saw her.

Friend, *El Roi* has not changed. He is the same yesterday, today, and forever. He sees *you.* He hears *you.* He knows *you* by name. If you want to read about Hagar's second encounter with *El Roi,* read Genesis 21.

☙ **As you ponder** *El Roi* **in your sacred silence, remember that He sees you sitting quietly at His feet. His gaze is upon you. He knows your name. He hears your cries. He not only notices your tears, but He collects them. He delights in your presence. He watches over you. He takes pleasure in every encounter with you. How does it comfort you to know God's eye is always upon you?**

_____

_____

_____

_____

Adonai Sal'i: God Our Rock

*pronounced *say-lie*

This name in Hebrew symbolizes an immovable foundation. It depicts God's constancy, strength, power, and presence. God is our solid foundation—unshakable—the underlying reality of all that we know to be good and true and real.

We find *Adonai Sal'i* in Hannah's story (1 Samuel 1:1–28). Hannah longed to have a child. Scripture tells us God had "closed her womb." In that day and time, the inability to conceive brought great shame.

Heartbroken and ashamed, Hannah humbled herself before God and prayed, "If you give me a child, I will give him back to You to serve You all the days of his life" (cf. 1 Samuel 1:11). Hannah so longed for a son that she was willing to give him back to the Lord.

What an example for us—to pray and seek God's help rather than allow our emotions to hold us hostage and drag us down to dark and desperate places!

God heard and answered Hannah's cry. Hannah gave birth to a son she named Samuel. When he was around age three, Hannah honored her deal with God, brought Samuel to the tabernacle, and gave him to the Lord.

Hannah prayed these words as she surrendered her child to God:

There is no one holy like the Lord;
there is no one besides you;
there is no Rock like our God. (1 Samuel 2:2)

The Voice translation says, "there is no rock *as solid* as our True God."

Hannah personally encountered God our Rock in a dark and desperate place. In Him she found strength, constancy, and unshakable confidence!

Here is great news! Hannah's God is our God. He is the same yesterday, today, and forever. So, when you're having a hard week or when you feel as if you're on sinking sand, you need only . . .

CRY OUT to the Rock.

STAND on the Rock.

PRAY to the Rock.

Pray this prayer: "Thank You, Lord, that You alone are my rock and my salvation, my fortress; I shall not be greatly shaken" (from Psalm 62:1–2).

🌿 **In your silent times with God, consider how *Adonai Sal'i* has made Himself known in your life and praise Him for His faithfulness. Or maybe you need Him right now. If you do, take time to ask Him if He will come and be your strength and confidence in what you're facing today.**

———————————————————————————————————————

———————————————————————————————————————

———————————————————————————————————————

As we close our time with the names of God, I thought I'd share one more way to keep God's names hidden in your heart—through prayer. One of my favorite ways to pray is opening my prayers by calling on God's name. I'll share one of my prayers by using the name Hagar gave God, *El Roi*, the God who sees.

My personal prayer:

El Roi, thank You that I'm never alone. There's no place I can go where You will not be with me. Thank You that when I stray, You see; when I'm lost, You find; when I'm hurt, You heal; when I'm empty, You fill; when I'm hungry, You feed; and when I fail, You restore. You are always near.

My prayer for you:

El Roi, draw close to Your daughter today. Remind her that You really do see her. All throughout her day, may she feel Your presence and experience Your love. Manifest Yourself to her in very real ways as You did to Hagar. Open the eyes of her heart to see You, hear You, and receive all that You have for her. I ask this in Jesus's name, amen.

LORD, REVEAL YOURSELF TO ME

I'm sure I'm not alone in questioning how God feels about me, especially when His silence and inactivity *feel* like He's saying, "I don't care." But what's even worse is when we come to *believe* God no longer cares—when we become utterly convinced God has forgotten us. That's what I witnessed the night our dear friends lost their twenty-year-old son, Richard, who was on duty fighting a fire.

Their story is hard. Richard had followed in his parents' footsteps, as Mike and Linay had both been firefighters. At the time of the fire, Richard was serving as a volunteer firefighter and was waiting to hear on his application to join the Charlotte Fire Department.

I'll never forget the night. My husband and I and a few friends (Richard's aunt and uncle) were enjoying a quiet night on our back porch. At one point, we heard sirens—so many that we even commented on how unusual it was. They sounded close—but then they faded. Our friends left, and we went to bed.

The next morning, I awoke to several text messages. The first relayed that Richard had been one of the firefighters called to that fire.

My first thoughts . . . how did I not hear those texts? Why didn't the Lord awaken me so I could have gone to the hospital? The last text crushed my heart, "Richard passed despite the doctor's best efforts." I reread those words again and again. Surely, this could not be. This precious boy we loved and watched grow up, gone, taken before he fully realized his greatest dream.

We spent the next several days greeting and serving the hundreds who dropped by with food and words of comfort. We coordinated media and the things that come along with planning a first responder's funeral service. There was no time to grieve, but only to serve and love. Love and serve.

Once the events passed and people stopped coming, reality set in. Richard was gone, and left in the wake of his loss were Mike, Linay, and Tyler (his sister), who adored him, as well as a huge extended family of grandparents, aunts, uncles, and cousins who deeply loved him. Their depth of loss and grief can't be put into words. You, too, may know this kind of grief.

A chaos of emotions erupted—especially about God. Anger with God. Confusion about His goodness and faithfulness, or His love. And, most of all, doubt about the truth of His Word.

Initially, Linay pressed in and drew closer to God. Mike, on the other hand, seemed to grow angrier and more distant. The unanswered questions were too hard for him to absorb.

However, what I witnessed in their marriage was beautiful. Each was taking care of the other. As Mike's faith waned and questioned, Linay's love and prayers held him up. When Linay's doubts crept in, Mike held her up. As for sweet Tyler, she was there for them both, sometimes setting aside her own grief to come alongside theirs.

What I witnessed most in Mike was skepticism about God's love and goodness. And isn't that natural? How can a good God take away a child from his parents? It's not the way things are supposed to be. My conversations with Mike revealed that he was headed down a path of believing wrong things—doubting God's love, provision, protection, and faithfulness. He was also thinking wrong things. *God doesn't care about me. God is not good if He's good with Richard's death. A loving God would not allow this.*

Each conversation left me grieved and frustrated. I sympathized, but I also desperately wanted to shake Mike, remind him of all the truths I knew that he knew, and make him align his thoughts with those truths.

But we can't do that for those whom we love. Grief is real. Grief is hard. Grief must be processed. Left unattended, grief will lie to us and blind us. And the longer it remains unattended, the deeper its tentacles grow.

There comes a time when the grieving one needs to put a stake in the ground. We can't do that for our loved ones. They have to come to that decision on their own. I saw Linay do just that.

Linay and I had been in Bible study together for years. Those years laid a foundation about who God is, His character, and His promises. That foundation provided the fertile ground in which Linay could plant her stake. When she shares their story, she testifies that God had gone before her and placed her in our study to prepare the way for this tragic chapter in her life.

Friend, we have a choice in whatever story God is writing. We can choose to put a stake in the ground or choose to sink deeper into grief and despair, fear and anxiety, and darkness and hopelessness. Only I can decide. Only you can decide. Only we can decide *who* and *what* reigns and rules over our hearts and minds.

Linay also made the intentional decision to remember God's past faithfulness. She continually reminded herself of the times God had been faithful in her life, in the lives of her loved ones, and most of all in the stories sitting in the pages of Scripture. She reminded herself of past answered prayers, the perfect verse sent at the perfect time, and the prayer prayed by a dear friend just when she needed it.

I know Linay would tell you that the best way to build trust in God's faithfulness is to know His character and understand the attributes that define who God is. Meditating on these is a wonderful, creative way to spend your silent time.

As we begin this journey of learning God's attributes, I pray that God expands your heart to receive more of who He is. I pray He uses this time to move the dark clouds hanging over you and the heaviness weighing upon you and walk you into His marvelous light!

WHY GOD'S ATTRIBUTES MATTER

An attribute is a quality, characteristic, or property that belongs to a person. So when we consider the attributes of God, we're answering questions like *Who is God? What is He like?* And maybe most relevant to our topic, *what kind of God is He?*

We learn about God's attributes through studying creation, Scripture, and Jesus. Even though we will never fully understand who God is because He is the Creator and we are His created ones, God created us to know Him. He knew we would be curious—He designed us to be curious. Because of this, He chose to make Himself known in many ways, most especially through His Word and His creation.

Pondering God's many attributes is another creative way to fix our eyes on Him in our times of silence because God's attributes point us to the beauty of *who* He is.

I most treasure these attributes during the times when I feel God has abandoned me, as I walk down the path of questioning what I believe about God. *Is He really good? Is He really in control? Is He really present? Does He even care?* These are the times that truly shift the solid ground beneath me.

Maybe you aren't there now, but you've been there in the past. Maybe you are reading this and can say, "That's me." The circumstances that lead us into our wilderness place may be different, but the emotions that compel us there are the same.

These emotions hold us hostage. They steal our peace and suffocate our joy. Only when we raise our hands in surrender can God begin His wilderness work in our souls. Surrender opens our hearts to receive from God. We can then travel the long and oftentimes winding road to rest, refreshment, and restoration, feasting on the Bread of Life and drinking from His sacred well of living water along the way.

Knowing God's attributes keeps us grounded in *who* God is, so we don't get lost in our disillusionment.

How do we land in these dark places? Sometimes it's because of our small view of God, shaped by past interactions with Him. The smaller God is in our eyes, the larger our pain and our problems seem. Other times, it may be because of flawed and wounded earthly parents who've hurt us. Still other times, it's because of many years of unanswered prayers. At least, I know that's how it is with me.

In the wilderness dark clouds move in, settle, and remain. They conceal the truth about God and obscure His goodness and glory, as well as His love and faithfulness.

Feeding ourselves fresh revelations of God's attributes equips us to effectively combat the lies and untruths we've been believing. The more we know and understand how big our God is, the more our pain and problems wane in comparison. It's called perspective.

Think about when you fly. As the plane's elevation increases, all that looms so large on the ground appears to shrink. Eighteen-wheelers look like Tonka trucks. Thirty-story skyscrapers look like Lego buildings. We know the trucks and skyscrapers have not actually changed in size; rather, our perspective has changed. Just as our view from an aircraft diminishes the size of objects on the ground, so our trust in the reality of a living and sovereign God changes our perspective on how we live and see our lives, especially when our trials and troubles feel larger than life.

Oh, it's true that our finite minds will never be able to take in the full greatness of who God is. But God has made it possible for our finite minds to step into His presence and receive glimpses of His glory through His many amazing attributes. Pondering those attributes in our sacred times of silence fuels our passion for more of God.

Are you ready for the next stop on our journey? Let's get to know God better together through His attributes.

GOD IS INFINITE, ETERNAL, AND SELF-EXISTENT

God said to Moses, "I AM WHO I AM. This is what you are to say to the Israelites: 'I AM has sent me to you.'" (Exodus 3:14)

God has no limits or boundaries. He's not confined to the dimension of space. God had no beginning. He has no end.

God is self-existent. God has no birthday and will never experience death. With God, everything that has ever happened or will ever happen has already occurred within His awareness. God encompasses all of eternity!

God expressed this attribute best in Exodus 3:14 when He appeared to Moses in a burning bush and announced that He was sending him to lead God's people out of slavery. Moses then asked God who He was. God's reply probably sounded strange to Moses: "I AM WHO I AM. This is what you are to say to the Israelites: 'I AM has sent me to you.'" Most scholars associate this Hebrew name of God, "I Am," with a form of the verb "to be" in the Hebrew language. It expresses God's self-existence— the fact that He transcends past, present, and future. While all created things exist because God created them, God exists outside of that created order because no one brought God into being and His existence depends on no one.

Though these are hard concepts to grasp, we can simply say that God has always been, He is, and He will always be. And, friend, for us this means that whatever we've been through, whatever we're walking through now, and whatever our future may hold, God is with us—and He is enough. Our infinite, eternal, self-existent *I Am* is enough for whatever burdens our hearts.

꩜ **What burdens your heart today? Invite I Am into your circumstances. Open your Bible and ask for Him to lead you to a word, verse, or passage so you can trust that He is big enough to take You through this. Remember, He knows what's waiting on the other side—He's already been there. Walk with Him.**

GOD IS IMMUTABLE: NEVER CHANGES

I the LORD do not change. (Malachi 3:6)

Malachi's words make it clear that God never changes. His nature, His essence, and His character all remain unchanged.

God is constant and consistent. His plans and His promises do not change. Scripture tells us in Hebrews 13:8 that God is the same yesterday, today, and forever. Immutable. Unchangeable for all eternity.

The book of James tells us, "Every good and perfect gift is from above, coming down from the Father of the heavenly lights, who does not change like shifting shadows" (1:17). This word "lights" in Greek is *phos* and means "light, a source of radiance." As specifically used here, it means a heavenly luminary (or star).

God's character—his goodness, love, faithfulness, and hope—is a constant like the stars in the sky. Yes, there are times we don't see the stars because clouds shroud them or the earth rotates on its axis away from them, bringing darkness. But the stars never stop shining brightly, even though we can't see them. It's the same with God—His love is constant and He is present with us. Circumstances may bring dark times or tragedy may cloud our judgment and cause us to question and turn away from God. But He is still there, bringing light into darkness and constancy into chaos.

What this means for us, friend, is that we have the comfort and confidence that our God is forever and always dependable. We can never make Him so angry nor can we do something so egregious that He will stop loving us. When my kids were little, my last words as I tucked them into bed were, "I love you more than the stars in the sky and the sands on the beach." My son especially loved that promise—he would often quote it back to me. Those words assured my kids how long and high, deep, and wide my love was for them. It was a love they could always count on, no matter what. Just like God's love.

God's love is constant, like the stars. He never stops loving us. His Word assures us in Romans 8:38–39 that *nothing* will ever separate us from His love . . . neither trouble nor hardship, neither danger nor persecution, neither death nor life, nor anything else in our past, present, or future. The bottom line is, no one and nothing in all creation will ever separate us from God's love in Christ Jesus! We are His beloved children, always.

🖉 **What feels like it's separating you from God? Read Romans 8:35–39. Ask God to bring that passage alive in your heart and help you to take Him at His word. Trust this promise from His heart to yours.**

GOD IS OMNIPRESENT: ALWAYS EVERYWHERE

> Am I a God at hand, declares the Lord, and not a God far away? Can a man hide himself in secret places so that I cannot see him? declares the Lord. Do I not fill heaven and earth? declares the Lord. (Jeremiah 23:23–24 ESV)

It's hard to wrap my mind around this attribute: God is present everywhere, in all spaces and places, in heaven and on earth. And it's not that God takes up space because God has no spatial dimensions. Because God is spirit, His makeup differs from any matter that we know. He has no weight and no height. He exists on a plane that reaches beyond our five senses.

Psalm 139 expresses this attribute beautifully:

> Where can I go from your Spirit?
>> Where can I flee from your presence?
> If I go up to the heavens, you are there;
>> if I make my bed in the depths, you are there.
> If I rise on the wings of the dawn,
>> if I settle on the far side of the sea,
> even there your hand will guide me,
>> your right hand will hold me fast. (vv. 139:7–10)

If I go up to the heavens

If I rise on the wings of the dawn

If I settle on the far side of the sea

If I make my bed in the depths

Reread this passage again, thinking about a cross as you read each verse. I wonder if that was God's intent as He breathed these words into the psalmist's heart—to take our minds to the cross with each verse.

God's love, Jesus's love, reaches everyone, everywhere. It's deep and wide and long and high. No one is too far from Him because He is everywhere! We cannot escape the reach of His love.

Verse 10 speaks most to my heart: "even there." Even in that sleepless night. Even in that hospital waiting room. Even in that job interview. Even when you sign the divorce papers. Even in *that*—those places you don't want to go, those places you don't want to be. God is still there with you—leading, guiding, loving, caring, protecting, and listening.

God also speaks of this omnipresence in a conversation with Jeremiah found in Jeremiah 23. What great comfort this passage brings to my heart, and I hope to yours! God is never far. So even when He feels distant He is near. Our God of all comfort, our God of hope, and our refuge and strong tower surrounds us right now, in this moment as we ponder this magnificent attribute. He is near.

⟡ **Take time to read Psalm 139 in its entirety. After you've read it, which words bring you the most comfort, and why? How do they help you where you are right now?**

GOD IS OMNISCIENT: ALL-KNOWING

> Oh, the depth of the riches of the wisdom and knowledge of God!
> How unsearchable his judgments,
> and his paths beyond tracing out!

"Who has known the mind of the Lord?
Or who has been his counselor?"
"Who has ever given to God,
that God should repay them?"
For from him and through him and for him are all things.
To him be the glory forever! Amen. (Romans 11:33–36)

God knows everything. Scholars use the word "omniscient" to describe this attribute of God. This Latin word comes from two terms: *scientia*, which means "knowledge," and *omni*, which means "all." God is "all-knowing."

The opening of John's gospel gives us greater insight into God's omniscience: "In the beginning was the Word, and the Word was with God, and the Word was God. He was with God in the beginning. Through him all things were made; without him nothing was made that has been made" (John 1:1–3).

God's knowledge goes beyond creation. Because God is everywhere (omnipresent), He sees all things. He never sleeps. His eyes are always upon the world and upon us. Every moment of every day He sees our every step. He knows our every thought. There isn't a place in this universe where God does not see and know.

He sees all those big life questions we have. He is aware of all the chaos, hatred, and violence ravaging our world and our nation. As believers, we know the One, the only One, who has the answers. We can take comfort that our omniscient God is always aware of everything.

James 1:5 instructs us where to go when we have these questions: "If you need wisdom, ask our generous God, and he will give it to you" (NLT). God is never surprised or bewildered because He's completely aware of *all* events past, present, and future.

In his book *The Knowledge of the Holy*, A. W. Tozer describes God's knowledge well:

Because God knows all things perfectly, He knows no thing better than any other thing, but all things equally well. He never discovers anything, He is never surprised, never amazed. He never wonders about anything nor (except when drawing men out for their own good) does He seek information or ask questions.[1]

◦ **I pray God's omniscience brings you great comfort today, because your all-knowing God is writing your story. It is a story He knows from birth to death. He was there in its beginning. He is with you now. He hears your cries and feels your pain. And because He is the author of your story, will you take one baby step toward trusting Him with the uncertainty of your tomorrows? Write these words somewhere where you will see them daily: "God, this is hard for me. But I'm choosing to trust You today. I will trust You because I know You are good. You are faithful. You know the future. You see me and are with me."**

GOD IS HOLY: SET APART

So you must live as God's obedient children. Don't slip back into your old ways of living to satisfy your own desires. You didn't know any better then. But now you must be holy in everything you do, just as God who chose you is holy. (1 Peter 1:14–15 NLT)

Scripture provides no greater witness of God's holiness than John's glorious glimpse of heaven in Revelation 4:

> Then as I looked, I saw a door standing open in heaven, and the same voice I had heard before spoke to me like a trumpet blast. The voice said, "Come up here, and I will show you what must happen after this." And instantly I was in the Spirit, and I saw a throne in heaven and someone sitting on it. The one sitting on the throne was as brilliant as gemstones—like jasper and carnelian. And the glow of an emerald circled his throne like a rainbow. Twenty-four thrones surrounded him, and twenty-four elders sat on them. They were all clothed in white and had gold crowns on their heads. From the throne came flashes of lightning and the rumble of thunder. And in front of the throne were seven torches with burning flames. This is the sevenfold Spirit of God. In front of the throne was a shiny sea of glass, sparkling like crystal.
>
> In the center and around the throne were four living beings, each covered with eyes, front and back. The first of these living beings was like a lion; the second was like an ox; the third had a human face; and the fourth was like an eagle in flight. Each of these living beings had six wings, and their wings were covered all over with eyes, inside and out. Day after day and night after night they keep on saying,"

> "Holy, holy, holy is the Lord God, the Almighty—
> the one who always was, who is, and who is still to come."
> (vv. 1–8 NLT)

Holiness is one of God's attributes and encapsulates God's absolute uniqueness. There is no one and no created thing like Him. God's beauty . . . His excellence . . . His purity . . . His worth are of infinite value.

We find another glimpse of God's holiness in Isaiah's vision in the book of Isaiah. The Hebrew word for "holy" as used here is *qadosh*, which means "separate, set apart, exalted." From what is God set apart? Creation. We talked about this earlier when we learned that God is self-existent. God is not a created being; He exists outside creation.

Spend a moment in the three verses that follow, soaking in what God so graciously allowed Isaiah to see and experience.

"I saw the Lord, high and exalted, seated on a throne; and the train of his robe filled the temple. Above him were seraphim, each with six wings: With two wings they covered their faces, with two they covered their feet, and with two they were flying. And they were calling to one another:

"Holy, holy, holy is the Lord Almighty;
the whole earth is full of his glory." (6:1–3)

We find much teaching about God's holiness here. First, the seraphim repeat the word "holy" three times. Why? Because repetition of words in the Hebrew language emphasizes and increases their intensity. They didn't say "holy" once or twice; they spoke it three times, emphasizing and declaring that God is holy to the highest possible degree.

Second, did you notice that in verse 3 Isaiah didn't say the whole earth is full of God's holiness? It says the whole earth is full of God's "glory." God's holiness put on display opens our eyes to see His glory. To bring this alive, let's look to Exodus 33 and see how God responded when Moses asked God to show him His glory: "'I will cause all my goodness to pass in front of you, and I will proclaim my name, the Lord, in your presence. I will have mercy on whom I will have mercy, and I will have compassion on whom I will have compassion" (v. 19). We find God's glory in His goodness, mercy, and grace toward us. Also, the heavens tell of His glory. And, finally, His creation and His created ones (that's us) reflect His glory.

God's glory is His holiness coming alive in our world and in our lives! Take some time to look around you. Where do you see God's glory? What is one way you can display God's glory this week?

_____

_____

_____

_____

_____

GOD IS WISE: PERFECT, UNCHANGING WISDOM

> How many are your works, LORD!
> In wisdom you made them all;
> the earth is full of your creatures. (Psalm 104:24)

We tend to think of wisdom as head knowledge. But wisdom is much more than that. A. W. Tozer provides a comprehensive definition of wisdom: "Wisdom, among other things, is the ability to devise perfect ends and to achieve those ends by the most perfect means. It sees the end from the beginning, so there can be no need to guess or conjecture. Wisdom sees everything in focus, each in proper relation to all, and is thus able to work toward predestined goals with flawless precision."[2]

Romans 11:33–36 describes God's wisdom:

> Oh, how great are God's riches and wisdom and knowledge! How impossible it is for us to understand his decisions and his ways!
>
> For who can know the LORD's thoughts?
> Who knows enough to give him advice?
> And who has given him so much
> that he needs to pay it back?

For everything comes from him and exists by his power and is intended for his glory. All glory to him forever! Amen. (NLT)

God spoke the entire universe into being. By His wisdom and creative power, it went from a "formless and empty" mass to a fully filled, gloriously perfect creation! God the master artist laid the foundations of the earth. His creative wisdom painted the horizons, set the heavenly bodies in position, and laid boundaries for the sea. He then formed and shaped living creatures, each created with its unique design and purpose. And, as His crowning creation, His masterpiece of all masterpieces, He created a creature in His own image. That, my friend, is you and me. We are image bearers of the One True God!

As you look at the world around you, what speaks most to you about God's wisdom? What comfort does this bring you when you walk through difficult times in your life?

_____

_____

_____

_____

_____

_____

_____

_____

GOD IS FAITHFUL: UNCHANGINGLY TRUE

Know therefore that the LORD your God is God; he is the faithful God, keeping his covenant of love to a thousand generations of those who love him and keep his commandments. (Deuteronomy 7:9)

Does this attribute remind you of one which we've studied? It takes me back to God's immutability. God never changes. Because He never changes, we can count on Him to always be faithful. The word faithful here is *aman* in Hebrew. It means "confirmed, established, sure."

I especially love this verse from Psalm 36:5: "Your steadfast love, O LORD, extends to the heavens, your faithfulness to the clouds" (ESV). God's words and promises are sure, established in the heavens. They are as sure as the rising and setting of the sun.

Unlike humans, God will never break a promise or change His mind. He has fulfilled every promise He made. We see this perfectly and beautifully reflected in the sending of His Son, our Savior Jesus.

John gave us a glorious vision of this truth in the book of Revelation: "I saw heaven standing open and there before me was a white horse, whose rider is called **Faithful and True** . . . on his [Jesus's] head are many crowns . . . His name is the Word of God . . . On his robe and on his thigh he has this name written: KING OF KINGS AND LORD OF LORDS" (19:11–16, emphasis mine).

Every word that God has spoken from Genesis to Revelation is rooted and grounded in His faithfulness.

My friends Joel Muddamalle and Lysa TerKeurst describe God's faithfulness well: "[O]ur God is a God of completion. He makes promises and then He fulfills them (Hebrews 10:23). Yes, the journey may be harder than we expected. The road to our promise may not look anything like we thought it would. But we can be rest assured there is never a question of whether our God will be faithful. Jesus is evidence of His faithfulness. We can trust Him . . . Our God is a promise-keeping God."[3]

If you're like me, you don't feel, and sometimes may even doubt, God's faithfulness when the plans playing out before you reflect nothing of His faithfulness. In fact, it may often seem just the opposite—like God has forgotten His promises and left you to fend for yourself.

Friend, in your doubt I want to remind you to look to God's Word and the stories that fill its pages. They will help you trust and endure, like they did for my friend Linay. You can press on because God has weaved stories of His faithfulness throughout the pages of Scripture. They reveal those who have gone before you and how they endured in the wait. You can also return to your own stories, or those of your friends, and trace God's hand of faithfulness.

🌀 **This tracing of God's handiwork in Scripture, and your own stories, assures you that He will be faithful again (Hebrews 10:35–36). Where have you seen God's faithfulness in your life? Take time now to reflect and respond to His faithfulness. Note what you remember in the space provided. Tuck those marked moments in your heart, so when you wonder where God is and if He even hears your prayers, you will remember that He was faithful before and will be faithful again.**

_____

_____

_____

_____

_____

_____

GOD IS GOOD

> Before I was afflicted I went astray,
> but now I obey your word.
> You are good, and what you do is good;
> teach me your decrees. (Psalm 119:67–68)

We often equate God's goodness with getting what we want or what we think is right. So when things go well we declare, "God is good" or "God is pleased with me." But when we find ourselves in the hard places we so desperately try to avoid, we question God's goodness and ask, "What did I do wrong? Why is God mad at me?"

These hard places mess with the truths we know and the lyrics we sing. It's hard to see friends in church with raised hands declaring, "He's a good, good Father," when God feels anything but good.

In these places, it's vital to remember that our circumstances don't accurately reflect God's goodness. Whether things go our way or not, God's goodness remains unchanged because it's rooted in His character. Always.

I encourage you to read Psalm 119:65–68 in its entirety. I chose it because we know by his word choice that the psalmist had walked through one of those dark places. We aren't given details, but we know that he walked away from God. We're also told that something happened in this dark place that led the psalmist back to God. More compelling is that the work God did in this hard place led him to obey God's Word.

Rather than grow bitter and resentful during that season, the psalmist came to realize two important truths about God: God is good and what God does is good. Because he came to believe both things were true, he asked God to teach him more. Because he entrusted his affliction to God, the psalmist came to know and experience God's goodness more deeply.

God's goodness saturates the pages of Scripture. The Psalms praise God's goodness (34:8, 100:5). Jesus affirms God's goodness in His conversation with the rich young ruler (Mark 10:18). Peter, too, spoke of God's goodness when he quoted Psalm 34:8 in 1 Peter 2:3.

☙ **If you find yourself questioning God's goodness, find a quiet place and sit with these verses. Read the words that come before and after them. Invite God to give you a fresh word about His goodness. I'm praying that God will take the truths you've gleaned and keep them close to your heart. The next time you doubt God's goodness, return to these Scriptures, following David's example in Psalm 16:2: "I say to the Lord, 'You are my Lord; apart from you I have no good thing.'"**

GOD IS LOVE: INFINITE, UNCHANGING LOVE

Dear friends, let us love one another, for love comes from God. Everyone who loves has been born of God and knows God. Whoever does not love does not know God, because God is love. This is how God showed his love among us: He sent his one and only Son into the world that we might live through him. This is love: not that we loved God, but that he loved us and sent his Son as an atoning sacrifice for our sins. Dear friends, since God so loved us, we also ought to love one another. (I John 4:7–11)

Yes, God loves us, and, yes, He is a loving God. But He's so much more. God *is* love. He's the very definition of love. Love is an intimate attribute that distinguishes our God from all other gods and religions. No other religion has sacrificial love as the driving force behind its beliefs. Love originates with God and is an integral part of His being. He is its source—its only source.

God gave breathtaking evidence of the height, width, depth, and length of His love by sending a living manifestation of it in Jesus. Jesus then gave testimony to the depth of His love for us when He willingly gave His life for ours and poured out His perfect, pure, holy blood on the cross at Calvary.

Beautiful gifts flow from this love:

Forever forgiveness (Romans 5:11; 8:1)
A new name . . . child of God (Galatians 3:26)
A new heart and a new spirit (Ezekiel 11:19; 2 Corinthians 5:17;
  Galatians 2:20)

God's Spirit in us, then, enables us to love in ways we never could in our own strength. R. C. Sproul expresses this well: "When we are transformed by the power of the Holy Spirit, we are given a capacity for this supernatural love that has God as its source and foundation."[4]

Friend, God has chosen *you* to be the earthly vessel He will use to reveal His love to this world. You have the honor and privilege of bringing God's love alive.

You are His ambassador.

⟲ **Friend, you are loved. God empowers you to live loved. Has God laid a name on your heart as you've learned more about His love? Pray and invite God to help you, in your own way, show His love to this person. Close with the following prayer.**

_____

_____

_____

_____

_____

_____

Father, thank You that You are love. And because I am Your child, Your love now lives in me. Through these struggles and my suffering, invade my heart with more of Your deep, unconditional, lavish love. I do trust that one day You will use this hard place, but right now it's difficult to see. Till that day, continue to reveal Yourself in my brokenness as I ponder and meditate on Your names and attributes. Move me forward step by step, day by day. Deepen my faith and trust. And when I'm ready, open a door for me to share Your love. I ask this in Jesus's name, amen.

GLORY: SPLENDOR AND BEAUTY

Lift up your heads, O gates!
And be lifted up, O ancient doors,
that the King of glory may come in.

161

Who is this King of glory?
The LORD, strong and mighty,
the LORD, mighty in battle! (Psalm 24:7–8 ESV)

God's glory incorporates the splendor of His attributes. Each one joined with another display the boundless beauty and magnificence of God's glory and perfection.

We daily witness God's glory in creation. The heavens declare the glory of the Lord (Psalm 19). God is clothed in glory and majesty (Psalm 104:1).

We experience God's glory in the stories sitting in the pages of Scripture: in the burning bush where God called Moses into leadership and confirmed his calling (Exodus 3:1–6); in the pillar of cloud by day and the pillar of fire by night reminding the Israelites that God was leading them (Exodus 13:21–22); in the tabernacle's Most Holy Place where God's very presence dwelled (Exodus 40:34–35); and in the bright cloud on the Mount of Transfiguration when God affirmed Jesus's identity as His Son (Matthew 17:1–6).

Add to all this Ezekiel's words describing God's glory:

And above that expanse over their heads was something that looked like a throne made of sapphire. Sitting on that throne high above the earth was a humanlike figure. From his waist up, I saw what looked to be glowing metal surrounded by an all-encompassing fire. Below his waist, I looked and saw something like a blazing fire. A glorious radiance was all around Him. The glorious radiance resembled a rainbow that lights up the clouds on a rainy day. This was nothing less than the glory of the Eternal that appeared to me. When I saw the vision of the Eternal and His glory, I fell upon my face and heard a voice speaking to me. (Ezekiel 1:26–28 The Voice)

Finally, we see God's glory displayed in all its fullness in Jesus. John painted a beautiful word picture: "The Word became flesh and made his dwelling among us. We have seen his glory, the glory of the one and only Son, who came from the Father, full of grace and truth" (John 1:14). The author of Hebrews also told us that Jesus is "the radiance of God's glory" (1:3).

Let's close with King David's words. May his words be ours as we ponder the glory and greatness of our Creator, Savior, and King in our sacred, silent time:

> Great is the LORD and most worthy of praise;
>   his greatness no one can fathom.
> One generation commends your works to another;
>   they tell of your mighty acts.
> They speak of the glorious splendor of your majesty—
>   and I will meditate on your wonderful works.
> They tell of the power of your awesome works—
>   and I will proclaim your great deeds.
> They celebrate your abundant goodness
>   and joyfully sing of your righteousness. (Psalm 145:3–7)

WHAT'S NEXT?

How can you assimilate what we've learned into your sacred times of solitude, silence, and prayer?

A few mornings a week, before you set your feet on the floor, take two or three minutes to greet the Lord and praise Him through His names and attributes. I'm sharing a prayer list of God's names and attributes to help you begin, and I encourage you to research and find more names and attributes. Each one that you learn will bring God alive in your heart in ways you never thought possible.

God, I praise You as,

King of Kings, Lord of Lords, Abba Father, Faithful and True, Lamb of God, Bread of Life, Living Water, Savior, Redeemer, Prince of Peace, Holy One, Comforter, Son of God, Good Shepherd, Alpha and Omega, Creator of Heaven and Earth, Defender, Strong Tower, Rock, Salvation, King of Glory, Strength of My Heart and My Portion Forever, Lover of My Soul, Rock of Ages, Emmanuel, Messiah, Name above All Names, The True Vine, Teacher, Light of the World, the Resurrection and the Life, the Great "I Am," the Same Yesterday, Today, and Forever!

God, I praise you as,

All-powerful, all-knowing, wise, holy, faithful, good, just, merciful, grace-filled, infinite, eternal, unchanging, ever-present, sovereign, righteous, loving, gracious, glorious.

I'll close with an update on Mike and Linay. Linay continued to cling to her faith, though very loosely on the hard days. She continued to show up and attend Bible study, even when she didn't feel like it. With each "yes," she watched God provide little by little everything she needed to turn her heart fully back to Him.

For Mike, it took more time. He wrestled through his feelings with friends and with one of our pastors who had lost his wife. Together they journeyed through grief using Scripture and focusing on God's character, truths, and promises. Little by little, Mike, too, opened his heart again to God. What's so beautiful is that he now realizes God never left him and was waiting with open arms to welcome him.

Are there hard days? Absolutely! But I've witnessed a deepened faith in both Mike and Linay. They've established a foundation in Richard's name and through it we provide for the needs of firefighters. They also come alongside and counsel other parents who have lost their loved ones fighting fires.

Today, Mike and Linay would both confess to you that even during their deepest loss and grief, God's character remains unchanged. God is good. Always. And He is true to His word in Romans 8:28. They know "that in all things God works for the good of those who love him, who have been called according to his purpose."

LORD, TEACH ME TO PRAY

oodness! I can't believe we're turning the final pages of this book, taking the last steps of our journey together. I'm thankful you've joined me. When God planted the seeds of this book in my heart, I didn't know your name. But God did. God had *you* in mind as He led me to write each word, craft each prayer, tell each story, and choose each verse. I love that! He knew we would be taking these final steps together.

I saved my favorite holy habit for last: prayer.

Have you ever found yourself desperate for the way life used to be before that *thing* happened? Before that person betrayed you? Before that doctor appointment? You prayed, desperate to hear God's voice. But all you heard was silence.

Maybe that describes you now.

Or maybe you pray but keep trying to fix what you're praying about even though you know it's beyond you to fix or change it.

When God doesn't seem to be answering your prayers, or even listening, it's hard—really hard.

Decades ago, I found myself in this very place and wrote these words:

God, I want my life back. I want this horrible nightmare to be over. I'm tired of living twenty-four hours a day in terror and fear. I want to be free to live the way I used to live before this man stole my life, my security, my joy, and my hope. But then tomorrow comes, God, and nothing changes. No matter what I pray or how many times I pray it, nothing changes. Where are you? Do you hear me?

Perhaps you're stuck in anger, fear, and doubt. Sadness and despair feel like they're swallowing your soul. That's when the "why" questions come rushing in.

All I wanted was a sign—any evidence that God was at work. I desired a peek into His plans or a whispered word from His heart. I wanted to feel His presence. I wanted His words of assurance that everything would turn out okay:

> Wendy, I hear you.
>> I have not forgotten you.
>> Take these steps.
>> Say these prayers. Read these verses and everything will be okay.

But I heard nothing.

I had a choice to make. I could believe what I was studying, reading, and learning, or I could allow anger, fear, and doubt to continue ruling my soul. What I came to realize during that time (though it was a decade-long journey) was that God was with me. And over those years, though my circumstances didn't always change, my courage to stand firm in them rose because I knew I was not alone. In His divine timing, God showed up in unimaginable, unfathomable ways.

I can't wait to share that story. But, first, let's talk about prayer.

THE HOLY HABIT OF SPENDING TIME IN PRAYER

Before Jesus came to earth, prayer looked very different. God's people, the Israelites, didn't have the same access to God that we have today.

They could only gain access through a priest, one very special priest chosen by God: the high priest. That priest could meet with God in only one place—the Most Holy Place (also called the holy of holies) in the tabernacle. A beautifully ornate curtain separated the Most Holy Place from the rest of the tabernacle. To learn more, read Exodus 25–28 and/or Exodus 35–40.

God made His home in the Most Holy Place, behind the veil. Only one person, the high priest, had authority to enter behind that veil (Hebrews 9:7). And then it was only for once a year to offer a perfect lamb, a blood sacrifice, to cover the sins of God's people. Without that sacrifice, God's people had no access to Him because sin (and the veil) stood in the way.

Well over a millennium later, because of His grace and great love for His people, God made a better way. He sent Jesus to be the ultimate sacrificial Lamb, thereby eliminating the need for the high priest's annual sacrifice. Jesus shed His blood to make a way for *all* people to have the opportunity to enter God's presence. Because of Jesus's sacrifice, the Israelites no longer needed high priests since Jesus had become the Great High Priest.

God graciously gives us a powerful picture of this moment in Mark 15:37–38: "With a loud cry, Jesus breathed his last. **The curtain of the temple was torn in two from top to bottom**" (emphasis mine).

Glory! Remain in this moment with me. What do you see? The searing of Jesus's flesh eliminated forever the veil, the last barrier between God and His people. That glorious, momentous moment in time changed everything. The author of Hebrews explained:

Therefore, brothers and sisters, since we have confidence to enter the Most Holy Place by the blood of Jesus, by a new and living way opened for us through the curtain, that is, his body, and since we have a great priest over the house of God, let us draw near to God with a sincere heart and with the full assurance [of] faith. (10:19–22)

Unlike the Israelites, God's people now have direct access to God anytime, anywhere. As children of the One True God, we not only have the right to stand in the presence of a Holy God, but we're also given the privilege to engage in a deep and abiding relationship with Him.

The question is, do we take advantage of this incredible access? Do we take advantage and boldly draw near, or do we fearfully linger just outside, never entering in?

Friend, God is waiting for you to draw near—to enter and discover what He has waiting for you on the other side. A beautiful, intimate, deep, and abiding prayer life awaits.

What does a deep and abiding prayer life look like?

I can't think of a more powerful way to answer this question than with my experience thirty-four years ago, long before I ever really read the Bible or had a meaningful relationship with God.

MY PRAYER STORY

Back in June 1986, I had just graduated from Baylor University and was newly engaged, with a wonderful job waiting for me. And then I experienced every woman's greatest fear. I entered my apartment to find an armed masked man waiting for me. He spent that afternoon sexually assaulting me and then walked out of my life. I never saw him again.

That day made me doubt everything I knew to be good and true. It made me doubt everything I had learned about God growing up—especially that He loved and cared about me.

After my attack, I prayed and asked God why He didn't intervene to stop what that man did to me. I asked Him to fix everything and make it better. I implored Him to take away the terror I lived with every day.

I heard nothing. Hours turned into days. Days turned into weeks. Weeks turned into years. I had good days where I opened my heart to God and expressed hesitant willingness to trust His timing. But on my not-so-good days, I reverted to anger, doubt, and confusion, wondering where God was . . . the One who said He loved and cared about me.

Twenty-eight years after my attack, God brought a woman named Elaine into my life to show me that He had been there every step of the way. He heard my desperate prayers. He had not forgotten me. He had not abandoned me. He was there—with me—always.

This providential encounter happened one weekend when I traveled to Houston, Texas, to speak at a women's conference.

After I finished sharing my testimony, I invited women to come up for prayer. During this prayer time, Elaine walked up, and I asked her how I could pray for her. She answered, "Oh, I don't need prayer. I have a story to tell you."

Elaine began by sharing that during her freshman year at Baylor, she had heard about a female student being raped. At that time, she was in a small group of students who prayed together. They made an intentional decision to pray for that student. They even prayed a specific passage of Scripture for her—Isaiah 62:1–4:

> For Zion's sake I will not keep silent,
>   for Jerusalem's sake I will not remain quiet,
> till her vindication shines out like the dawn,
>   her salvation like a blazing torch.
> The nations will see your vindication,
>   and all kings your glory;
> you will be called by a new name
>   that the mouth of the LORD will bestow.
> You will be a crown of splendor in the LORD's hand,
>   a royal diadem in the hand of your God.
> No longer will they call you Deserted,
>   or name your land Desolate.
> But you will be called Hephzibah,
>   and your land Beulah;

for the Lord *will take delight in you,*
and your land will be married.

Now, if I had read or known that passage at the time, I wouldn't have understood a single word because it's Old Testament stuff about Jerusalem that would have gone completely over my head.

Elaine texted her husband to send a screenshot of her Bible opened to the Isaiah 62 passage. Written on that yellowed page, next to the Isaiah passage, I saw my name and the year 1986. Even typing my words here brings tears to my eyes.

Elaine had come to that conference having no idea I was *that* Wendy. I had gotten married, so my last name was different. I was living in Charlotte, not Texas. Even after she arrived at the conference, she still had no idea who I was.

During the message, when Elaine heard me describe how I felt forsaken by God, she said that tears came to her eyes because "forsaken" was the exact word used in the passage they had prayed for me.

She texted her husband again and asked him to find and send the page in her prayer journal from that year. She had taken the Isaiah 62 passage and personalized it for me. We'll learn how to do that later in this chapter.

God, for Wendy's sake I will not keep silent, and for her soul I will not keep quiet, until Wendy's righteousness goes forth like brightness and Wendy's salvation is like a torch that is burning. The nations will see Wendy's righteousness, and everyone will see her glory. And Wendy will be called by a new name which the mouth of the Lord will designate; Wendy will be a crown of beauty in the hand of the Lord and a royal diadem in the hand of You, God. It will no longer be said of, about, or by her that she is **Forsaken** *nor will her soul, her spirit, or her name be called Desolate. But Wendy will be called, "my delight is in her" . . . and God will rejoice over Wendy, and she will be glad.*

I wept again and realized in that moment that God had never once forgotten me. Not only had He not forgotten me, but He had also appointed Elaine and her friends to pray for me when I couldn't pray for myself. When I was angry with God—doubting Him, rejecting Him, cursing Him—He never walked away.

How good and sweet God is! I know that God didn't have to give me this beautiful glimpse of His handiwork. But He did. I love that He cared enough to reach down from the heavens, arrange this divine appointment, and again remind me that He is *El Roi*, the God who sees, and *Jehovah Jireh*, the God who provides. He is the God who is Faithful and True. Always.

Maybe you feel like how I was all those years ago. You want everything to be over and done with. But you can't. It isn't over.

No matter what you say or pray, nothing works. Nothing changes. You're a tangled mess of emotions, and "why" questions keep tumbling in.

If you're there, hear these words and let them sink in: Jesus is near. He's as near as your next breath. You need only call on His name. *Jesus*.

꩜ **Take a break here. If you need Jesus, He is near. Be still. Call out His name. Be still. Speak His name again. Jesus. Jesus. He is near. Take a few minutes to remain here. Write what God lays on your heart.**

Jesus invites us, "Come to me, all you who are weary and burdened, and I will give you rest" (Matthew 11:28). He may not fix everything at that moment. In fact, He probably won't. But it's an invitation to come and sit with the only One who can give you rest in the middle of the mess.

That's what this chapter is about—accepting the invitation to pray and knowing what to do and how to do it once we accept it.

Although there is no one correct way to pray, I've learned some valuable lessons as I've traveled this long journey to understand and deepen my prayer life. Let's call them guidelines for prayer as we begin.

1. PRAY TO GOD

Call on God by name as you pray. One way I do this is by praying the names of God we've studied.

We see this modeled in both the Old and New Testaments (emphases mine throughout this section).

First Kings 18:36 says, "the prophet Elijah stepped forward and prayed: 'Lord, **the God of Abraham, Isaac and Israel** . . .'"

In Matthew 6:9, Jesus teaches us how to pray: "This, then, is how you should pray: '**Our Father in heaven** . . .'"

In 2 Samuel 7:27–28, David prayed, "**Lord Almighty**, **God of Israel**, you have revealed this to your servant, saying, 'I will build a house for you.' So your servant has found courage to pray this prayer to you. **Sovereign Lord**, you are God! Your covenant is trustworthy, and you have promised these good things to your servant."

I hope you noticed the many magnificent names of God in these verses. Lord. God of Abraham, Isaac, and Israel. Father. Lord Almighty. Sovereign Lord.

2. PRAY IN THE NAME OF JESUS

James taught in James 5:14, "Is anyone among you sick? Let them call the elders of the church to pray over them and anoint them with oil **in the name of the Lord**."

John 14:13 says, "And I will do whatever you **ask in my name**."

When we pray in Jesus's name, we aren't simply reciting or

mentioning His name. We pray in accordance with all that Jesus's name represents and the power it carries. We pray a prayer that will carry forward the work He did while on this earth.

3. PRAY IN FAITH

James 5:15 says, "And the prayer **offered in faith** will make the sick person well."

Hebrews 11:1 says, "Now faith is confidence in what we hope for and assurance about what we do not see."

Romans 10:17 says, "Faith comes from hearing the message, and the message is heard through the word about Christ."

Paul made clear in Romans 10:17 that the more time we spend in God's Word, the more our faith increases. The more our faith increases, the more faith-filled our prayers will be.

To recap, we pray to God, in Jesus's name, in faith.

Let's linger a bit at our next guideline.

4. PRAY ACCORDING TO GOD'S WORD

In his devotion book *You Can Count on God*, Max Lucado gives great insight into what it looks like to pray God's Word:

> God invites you—yes, commands you—to remind him of his promises. . . . Find a promise that fits your problem and build your prayer around it. These prayers of faith touch the heart of God and activate the angels of heaven. Miracles are set into motion. Your answer may not come overnight, but it will come. And you will overcome.[1]

First Thessalonians 2:13 says, "And we also thank God continually because, when you received the word of God, which you heard from us, you accepted it not as a human word, but as it actually is, **the word of God, which is indeed at work in you who believe.**"

Romans 9:28 says, "For the Lord will **execute His word** on the earth, thoroughly and quickly" (NASB).

Isaiah 55:10–11 says, "As the rain and the snow come down from heaven, and do not return to it without watering the earth and making it bud and flourish, so that it yields seed for the sower and bread for the eater, **so is my word that goes out from my mouth: It will not return to me empty, but will accomplish what I desire and achieve the purpose for which I sent it.**"

Jeremiah 1:12 says, "The LORD said to me, 'You have seen correctly, for **I am watching to see that my word is fulfilled.**"

Praying God's Word ensures that our prayers will be powerful and effective. Why? Because when God's living and active Word fills our hearts and minds, it conditions and controls our prayers in such a way that they will conform to His will and therefore be effective.

Does that make sense?

Let me say it again: When God's living and active Word fills our hearts and minds, it will condition and control our prayers in such a way that our prayers will conform to His will and therefore be effective.

Let's review the guidelines we've covered. We pray to God, in Jesus's name, in faith, according to God's Word.

5. PRAY WITH CONFIDENCE

Abiding in God's Word fills us with His Word. That filling increases our faith. And our increased faith helps us pray more confidently.

John 15:7 says, "If you remain in me and my words remain in you, ask whatever you wish, and it will be done for you."

John tells us that if we abide in Jesus and His Word is in us, we can ask what we wish and it will be done for us. Now, let's add verse 8. Why will God answer those "abiding in" Him prayers?

This is to my Father's glory, that you bear much fruit, showing yourselves to be my disciples.

I want to stop here for a moment to answer a question you may be asking: What about when we pray according to God's Word and will, and God still doesn't answer our prayers? Does that make God less trustworthy or His Word untrue?

I've asked these questions and been asked them many times. The answer requires a deeper understanding of "unanswered prayers."

God commands us to pray, not to grant our wishes or give us our way. Rather, God commands us to pray to build a relationship with Him and deepen our faith and trust in Him. I can't think of a better person to answer this question about unanswered prayers than Jesus. He set the very best example in the garden of Gethsemane when He cried out to His Father, "Father, if you are willing, take this cup from me; yet not my will, but yours be done" (Luke 22:42).

Before I share my thoughts, Charles Spurgeon brings great wisdom regarding our questions and this scene:

> Having been found in fashion as a man, [Jesus] humbled Himself and became obedient to His Father's will. Now, obedience is not perceived until it is tried, and faith is not known to be firm and strong until it is put to the test and exercised.[2]

Pause and read Spurgeon's words again: "Obedience is not perceived until it is tried" and "faith is not known to be firm and strong until it is put to the test and exercised." Ouch! Those words step on my toes, and it doesn't feel good.

Now, back to Spurgeon's words as he explains further:

> Through what an ordeal did this pure gold pass! It was put into the crucible and thrust into the hottest coals, all glowing with a white

heat, they were heaped upon Him, and yet no dross was found in Him. His faith never staggered. His confidence in His God never degenerated into suspicion and never turned aside into unbelief. It is, "*My* God! *My* God!" even when He is forsaken.

It is, "*My God and my strength*" even when He is poured out like water and all His bones are out of joint. In this thing, He not only sympathizes with us, you see, but *He sets us an example*. We must overcome, as He did, through faith. "This is the victory which overcomes the world, even your faith." And if we can copy this great High Priest of our profession, who endured such contradiction of sinners against Himself—if we can copy Him so as to be neither faint in our minds, nor turn from our Master's work—we shall triumph even as He overcame.[3]

Friend, on the days we struggle with unanswered prayer, let's fix our eyes on Jesus. Remember, in Jesus's humanity He identifies with us. He went before us. He set the example to follow. And if that isn't enough, we've learned that through His Holy Spirit we have the strength and the power to follow in His footsteps. So when we don't see God answering our prayers as we ask, draw nearer, my friend. Wait on Jesus. He has gone before you in this place, and He's walking with you now. And He will meet you on the other side.

Jesus's prayers in both the wilderness and the garden teach us how to pray. Jesus prayed prayers:

- led by the Spirit
- formed with God's words
- conformed to God's will

And while we wait on God's answer, let's agree to never stop trusting, never cease praying, and never give up hope.

I have a question for you before we move on to our next guideline. Are you afraid to pray? If so, why?

Are you afraid your prayers are inadequate?

Are you afraid your prayers aren't eloquent enough?

Or maybe you're like me. For many years I didn't pray because I couldn't pray with the same depth and faith as other people.

Read these next words carefully. Soak them in. I write them from personal experience!

The trust in God,

the confidence,

the depth,

the eloquence,

the richness,

and the passion you feel, see, and hear in other people's prayers flows from their abiding hearts. Men and women who pray like that aren't special people. They're simply people who pray what already fills their hearts.

Dear friend, God isn't judging or grading your prayers. God doesn't care about the number of words or the way in which you pray them. He just wants to hear sincere prayers from His children. There truly is no right or wrong way.

I want to be sure that you hear me. I'm sharing *guidelines* to *deepen* your prayer life. They are not rules you must follow. Laying God's promises before Him helps you pray more confidently and effectively. My hope is that you'll walk away with the confidence to boldly pray for the desires of your heart—not centered solely on the answer you want but for God's will to be done!

Let's add a few more guidelines to our prayer process. So far, we pray to God, in Jesus's name, in faith, according to His Word, with confidence.

6. PRAY PERSISTENTLY AND EARNESTLY, WITH ANTICIPATION

Scripture continually encourages us to pray this way:

*Devote yourselves to prayer, being watchful
and thankful. (Colossians 4:2)*

Pray continually. (1 Thessalonians 5:17)

*And pray in the Spirit on all occasions with all kinds of
prayers and requests. With this in mind, be alert and always
keep on praying for all the Lord's people. (Ephesians 6:18)*

We studied this earlier in this chapter. It is devoted, continual, persistent prayer.

Let's review one more time before we move to our last guideline. We pray to God, in Jesus's name, in faith, according to His Word, with confidence, persistently and earnestly, with anticipation.

7. PRAY SPECIFICALLY

We often hesitate to pray specifically. Maybe because we question our motives. Maybe because we wonder if what we're praying is in God's will. Maybe because we don't see prayers answered like they were in the Bible. Maybe we wonder if God's miracles aren't for our day and time.

Friend, the problem isn't with God—it's with us. Quite often, we simply don't ask.

God filled the pages of Scripture with stories of specific answered prayers. These prayers applied many of the same guidelines we're learning. There are examples after examples of people who prayed to God in faith, according to His Word, and with confidence. They prayed persistently and earnestly, with anticipation. And so should we. When we do this, we will see God at work in our midst.

These saints also prayed specifically, whether it was for a child, a sign, or a miracle. Or perhaps they asked for a healing, a direction, or a confirmation. They asked God for exactly what they wanted.

I pray that what we've learned moves you to go to God with your requests, just as children go to their fathers with theirs. It truly is God's pleasure to give good gifts to you and to answer your prayers when you've surrendered them to His purposes and aligned them with His wisdom.

First John 5:14–15 says, "This is the confidence we have in approaching God: that if we ask anything according to his will, he hears us. And if we know that he hears us—whatever we ask—we know that we have what we asked of him."

I shared the following story in my first book, *Hidden Joy in a Dark Corner*. I'm sharing it again here because it's a beautiful and powerful example of specific prayer.

My dear friend's daughter, Frances, presented some very concerning symptoms at age two. She was bloated, gaining weight, and had trouble urinating. One night, she reached a point where they had to rush her to the emergency room. Doctors diagnosed her with nephrotic syndrome. In simple terms, her damaged kidneys were leaking large amounts of protein into her body. Her inability to urinate had caused toxins to build, poisoning every part of her tiny body. Even when the doctors stabilized her, she was unable to flush her body of the toxins naturally. Fearing that Frances wouldn't make it through the night, they ordered dialysis as a last resort.

Frances hated dialysis. She required multiple treatments day and night, and she screamed through each one. It was unbearable watching this precious toddler fight to pull out the very tubes that kept her alive. One evening when Frances saw the nurse walk in to set up the machine, she lost it. We had to forcibly hold her down. It was agonizing. I wept as my hands held her down. She looked into my eyes, wailing and writhing in pain.

In a desperate moment, Karen cried out from the depths of her mother's heart, "Let her pee, Father." We began calling on everyone to pray this three-word prayer. One afternoon at the hospital, I sat with Karen, holding Frances in my lap while Karen wrapped up a phone conversation. As I held Frances, the Lord led me to place my hand on her belly. I began to fervently pray for healing in her kidneys and for perfect functioning to be restored.

As I prayed, my hand grew strangely warm . . . then warmer . . . it began to flush with redness . . . and then it felt fiery hot. I placed Karen's hand on mine, and tears began to flow as we saw God's very power in our presence. In that moment, we believe our prayer joined thousands of others being lifted for Frances in supernaturally powerful and effective ways.

What happened next was nothing short of a miracle! When Frances awakened, the nurses found a soaking wet diaper! Frances had urinated on her own with no machine and no drugs. Her wet diaper served as a glorious testimony of God's healing power and faithfulness. What doctors earlier in the week claimed was a medical impossibility became a medical reality. Doctors could not explain what happened that incredible night, but we could—and did!

Friends, as we close, here are two truths to be assured of when we pray.

First, God never does nothing in answer to our prayer.

Even when it seems that God says "wait" and/or "no" to our specific prayer, it doesn't mean He isn't working and moving in response to it. Let's return to Matthew 7 to dig a little deeper. We can look at verses 9–11 to see how God responds to our prayers:

> Ask and it will be given to you; seek and you will find; knock and the door will be opened to you. For everyone who asks receives; the one who seeks finds; and to the one who knocks, the door will be opened.
>
> Which of you, if your son asks for bread, will give him a stone? Or if he asks for a fish, will give him a snake? If you, then, though you are evil, know how to give good gifts to your children, how much

more will your Father in heaven give good gifts to those who ask him! (vv. 7:7–11)

Matthew used some creative analogies in verses 9–11. But the preceding verses we studied earlier (verses 7 and 8) are specific invitations —commands, really—to come to Him with our needs. Ask. Seek. Knock. I think Jesus wants to be sure we know He's serious about this prayer thing. It's why He says it three times, three different ways. Ask. Seek. Knock. Jesus means what He says.

The promises Jesus gives when we obey the command to pray are also specific. Ask and *it will be given.* Seek and *you will find.* Knock and *the door will be opened.* Everyone who asks *receives.* Everyone who seeks *finds.* Everyone who knocks *finds an open door.* God will act when we pray. He will answer. He will give good things when we pray.

John Piper expounds on this teaching:

> If we take the passage as a whole, it says that when we ask and seek and knock—when we pray as needy children looking away from our own resources to our trustworthy heavenly Father—he will hear and he will give us good things. Sometimes just *what* we asked. Sometimes just *when* we ask it. Sometimes just *the way* we desire. And other times he gives us something better, or at a time he knows is better, or in a way he knows is better.[4]

I'm not sure if you noticed Jesus's specific word choice in verse 11. God promises to give good things to His children *"who ask."* We must ask! It's also a telling word choice, because Jesus *doesn't* say He gives us what we ask for. He says that when we ask, He gives us "good gifts" (v. 11). These good gifts might look different from what we've envisioned and/or prayed. But our good God, even more than parents, knows what's best for His children (us) and sometimes the answer "wait," or even "no," is what's best.

Second, God is sovereign. When we pray, we must remember that we pray to a sovereign God. We spent time on this attribute of God in an earlier chapter. Our Sovereign God is the One who is the Blessed Controller of all that happens on this earth and in our lives. He has a plan and purpose for every life, though in the moment it may not feel like it. It's a good plan—a perfect plan. And as we walk with Him, He invites— no, He commands—us to pray in faith without doubting, trusting that He is a good God and will do His good will. Always.

☞ **What prayer has been on your heart? What prayer have you been afraid to pray? Friend, take time now to pray using some of the guidelines we learned. Whether you pray in your spirit or write it on paper or type it in your phone, lay your prayer before the Lord and hold back nothing, remembering what we learned. Pray to God, in Jesus's name, in faith, according to His Word, with confidence, persistently and earnestly, with anticipation, and pray specifically. Don't "one and done pray" your prayer. Keep it ever before you, waiting and watching for God to be at work.**

WHEN WE PRAY, WHAT SHOULD WE PRAY?

Do you struggle with knowing what to pray and how to pray? I can relate!

Sometimes it's hard to know where to begin with prayer. You want to pray specifically, but you can't quite figure out how to do it.

My prayer life changed when I served on a Bible study leadership team who taught me to pray God's Word. This change transformed my prayer life. It helped me to pray more confidently, and I can't wait to share what I learned with you!

Why Does Praying God's Word Make Our Prayers More Powerful and Effective?

Think about these two questions:

Mom, can I have a piece of candy?

Mom, remember yesterday when you promised me a piece of candy? May I have it now, please?

Which statement probably resonates more strongly in a mom's heart? The one in which her child simply asks for a piece of candy, or the one in which her child *reminds* her of *her* promise to give him a piece of candy.

☙ **Take a moment with this question. As you ponder and answer it, consider your prayer life with God. How do you pray when you're asking God for something?**

_____

_____

_____

As a mom, I can tell you the latter question resonated more strongly with me. That's how prayer works. When we pray God's Word back to Him, we're *reminding* Him of His promises.

What the Bible Says about God's Word

I've taught on this topic often, whether in books or on a stage. It's one of my most requested teachings because the principles from God's Word on prayer never change!

The Bible gives us a great promise about God's Word in Hebrews 4:12:

For the word of God is alive and active. Sharper than any double-edged sword, it penetrates even to dividing soul and spirit, joints and marrow; it judges the thoughts and attitudes of the heart.

🗘 **What words does the author use to describe God's Word?**

Let's study the meaning of three of these words.

First, God's Word is "living."

Some translations use the word "quick." This word is from the Greek word *zao*, which means "to live, to be alive, to have vital power in itself and exert the same upon the soul." God's Word is not a dead piece of literature to be read, enjoyed, and put back on the shelf. It's relevant to our lives today. This implies God's Word is inexhaustible, meaning no amount of study can deplete its potential to impact and influence our lives. Every time we open His Word, God is waiting to speak a fresh word from His heart to ours. But God's voice must feel familiar to us if we are to hear Him speak. We need to recognize and know His voice.

This is where another sacred pause comes into play. It's important to spend time in God's Word and take time to listen for His voice as we read and study. Friend, it's in our reading, studying, and listening that God speaks, leads, guides, convicts, encourages, and ministers to our hearts.

Second, God's Word is "active."

Some translations use the word "powerful." This word is from the Greek word *energes*, which means, "effective, productive of due result, at work." By using this word, the author of Hebrews ensured that we know God intends for His Word to cause activity and change in our lives. We witness this activity throughout the Bible. When God's Word was spoken through Jesus and His disciples, it convicted people of their sin; converted their hearts; raised the dead to life; and made the deaf to hear, the blind to see, the mute to speak, and the lame to walk.

Third, God's Word is "sharper."

The author of Hebrews emphasized the sharpness of God's Word: "sharper than any double-edged sword." This word "sharper" is from the Greek word *tomoteros*, meaning "to cut with a single stroke," as opposed to hacking away with repeated blows. God wants to use His Word to seize us immediately and quickly. It cuts to the heart of the issues we're struggling and praying about, and then penetrates us deeply. It reaches into the depths of our hearts and souls, even into the very marrow of our bones, to effect change in our lives.

Jesus teaches us more about prayer in John 15.

☞ **Read John 15:1–16. How many times do you see the word "remain," "abide," or "joined" (depending on your translation)? What image do these words conjure up, and how does that image connect with prayer? Do Jesus's words reflect your prayer life? If so, why? If not, why not?**

_____

_____

_____

_____

_____

_____

When teaching His disciples about abiding and prayer, Jesus spoke these words:

If you remain in me and my words remain in you, ask whatever you wish, and it will be done for you. This is to my Father's glory, that you bear much fruit, showing yourselves to be my disciples. (John 15:7–8)

🕉 **Jesus says to "remain" in Him. What does "remaining" in Jesus look like in your life?**

_____

_____

_____

_____

_____

_____

_____

_____

_____

On a trip to Israel, I learned that some scholars believe Jesus's conversation with His disciples in John 15 took place while they walked through or past an actual vineyard. If that's the case, while Jesus explained that He was the True Vine and His followers were the branches, they could have been looking upon abundant vines bursting forth with fruit. How cool is that?

The first part of verse 7 invites us to *remain (abide)* in Christ. Remaining or abiding simply means spending time with Jesus in His presence and in His Word. The more time we spend with Jesus, the more His Word stimulates and permeates our hearts and minds. The more steeped we are in God's Word, the more it becomes a part of us and the more the fruit of His Spirit—love, joy, peace, patience, kindness, goodness, faithfulness, gentleness, and self-control—comes fully alive in us (Galatians 5:22–23).

The second part of the verse tells us that when we remain in God's Word, whatever we ask will be given.

This is *not* telling us that when we pray we will for sure get exactly what we pray for. God is not a genie in a bottle—we talked about this earlier.

Receiving what we ask in prayer requires a close, intimate, interactive relationship with Jesus. The key to this is listening with a discerning heart as you read God's Word. This intimacy and listening enables you to hear God's voice. The more you hear it, the more you'll recognize it. His words and voice become familiar.

What we're studying is incredibly important to one of the most often-asked questions in prayer: "God, what is Your will?" We find God's will in His Word. Romans 12:2 makes this clear: "Do not conform to the pattern of this world, but be transformed by the renewing of your mind. Then you will be able to test and approve what God's will is—his good, pleasing, and perfect will."

So, connecting this with what we just learned, the more familiar we are with God's Word, the more familiar His voice will feel. The more familiar His voice, the easier it becomes to discover His will. The more familiar we are with His will, the easier it becomes to align our hearts with His will. And the more we align our hearts with His will, the more our prayers begin to reflect, and be driven by, His Word and His will.

Now let's get more specific on how to pray God's Word.

Baby Steps to Praying God's Word

Let's get practical. How exactly do we pray God's Word?

I'll begin by sharing how I learned to pray God's Word and then invite you to join me.

Step One: Find Your Verse and Personalize It

First, I find something weighing heavily on my heart and invite God into this process. I'll share what I pray using Psalm 119:18, which says, "Open my eyes that I may see wonderful things in your law."

My prayer, praying Psalm 119:18, is this: *Father, open the eyes of my heart so I can find what You want to speak to me about* _____.

Second, I turn to the concordance at the back of my Bible. A concordance organizes Scripture by topic (fear, worry, peace, forgiveness, anger, peace, joy, etc.). Another quick way to find a verse by topic is to do a Google search. Type in the search bar "find Bible verse on _____." I then take the verse I find and jot it down in a journal or notebook or type it into a document. I again ask God for ears to hear and a heart to receive what He wants to speak to me through the verse to which He led me.

Finally, I personalize and pray each verse as God leads. I'll share some examples.

At a time when I wanted to pray for my children but wasn't quite sure what to pray or how to do it, I went to God's Word. I took baby steps and found a few Scriptures that spoke to what was on my heart. I then personalized them.

A FEW EXAMPLES

First, I'll share the verse the Lord gave me. Next, I'll invite you to find the verse, read it, and write it. Finally, I'll show you how I personalized it.

◌ **Find, read, and write Philippians 4:6–7 and Isaiah 26:3.**

My personalized prayer using Philippians 4:6–7 and Isaiah 26:3:

> *May Lauren be anxious for nothing. In everything may she bring her worries and concerns to You, Lord, so that Your peace that passes all understanding will guard her heart and mind. Keep her heart steadfast and trusting in You always.*

�✎ **Find, read, and write Joshua 1:7.**

_____

_____

_____

_____

_____

_____

My personalized prayer using Joshua 1:7:

> *Father, help Bo be strong and very courageous. Help him to obey You in all that he says and does. May he never turn to the left or to the right, but keep His eyes fixed on You so that he may be successful wherever he goes and whatever he does.*

�✎ **Find, read, and write Luke 2:52.**

_____

_____

_____

_____

_____

My personalized prayer using Luke 2:52:

> *Father, grow Lauren and Bo in wisdom, stature, and favor with You and with man.*

NOW IT'S YOUR TURN

Since most of us struggle with worry and anxiety at one time or another, I thought that would be a great topic to begin this section.

Take a few minutes to find the words *anxious, anxiety, worry,* or *peace* in your Bible's concordance (or use Google). Prayerfully read through the verses you find.

Listen for God's voice. By this, I mean pay attention to words that stir your soul or strike a chord with what's on your heart. That's usually how you know God is answering your prayer to "open the eyes of your heart" to receive what He has for you. I usually find two to four verses.

🌀 **Once you find your verse(s), write each one here.**

_____

_____

_____

_____

🌀 **Now take some time to personalize each verse.**

_____

_____

_____

_____

Step Two: Weave Your Verses into a Prayer

After you find and personalize your verses, the next step is to pray them. You can do this verbally, of course. But what helped grow my prayer life the most was taking my verses and weaving them together into a longer written prayer. Imagine as you craft your prayer that you're stringing pearls together (remember that we talked about stringing pearls when we memorized Scripture?) to create a beautiful prayer necklace.

Two of my favorite verses on peace are Philippians 4:6–7 (used in my daughter's prayer earlier) and Isaiah 26:3 (one of our memory verses):

> *Don't worry about anything; instead, pray about everything.*
> *Tell God what you need, and thank him for all he has done.*
> *Then you will experience God's peace, which exceeds anything*
> *we can understand. His peace will guard your hearts and*
> *minds as you live in Christ Jesus. (Philippians 4:6–7 NLT)*

You will keep in perfect peace
those whose minds are steadfast,
because they trust in you. (Isaiah 26:3)

Next, you'll see how I personalized these two verses (pearls) to weave (string) them together into a beautiful prayer (necklace).

I begin sharing with God what's on my heart, and then I pray the Scriptures into and over my circumstances:

Father, I have so much on my mind right now. I can't sleep. I feel so anxious. Your Word tells me to fix my mind on You, not on my circumstances and my worries. Your Word tells me to pray about everything. So, right now, I'm coming to You with my worries, especially the fact that I can't rest or relax. It feels like a motor is constantly running in my body. My mind never stops. I desperately want to walk in the fullness of Your peace.

So, Father, I thank You that I can stop trying to control everything because You are in control of all things. I'm choosing to fix my mind on You and Your promises. I'm doing this so that You will make my heart steadfast. And I'm giving all my worries to You, claiming Your promise that Your peace, the peace that passes all understanding, will guard my heart and mind. I trust You for this peace because You are a promise-keeping God. I thank You that as I continue to fix my eyes on You and trust You with my circumstances, I will be filled with Your peace from the top of my head to the tips of my toes. I trust You and will wait patiently as You heal me and grant me rest from the inside out. In Jesus's name I pray, amen.

NOW IT'S YOUR TURN TO WRITE YOUR PRAYER

For this section, you'll need your Bible, a pen, and a notebook/journal/paper or your computer (to write your verses and your prayer).

As we begin, keep these words in mind: No matter what the

challenge before you may be, the Bible contains truths and promises to speak to your circumstances. In fact, the Bible contains thousands of promises, each one breathed into its pages by God for a special time or specific need. Ingesting, studying, memorizing, and learning these truths and promises keeps them hidden in your heart. Once digested, they become living and active healing, hope-filled words for even your darkest hours.

Sometimes it's hard to find these promises, so I thought I'd get you started. In the next section you'll find a variety of topics, along with Scriptures that address these topics. Prayerfully read through them. Choose one topic that speaks to your heart. It may be for you or someone you love.

The topics include:

- Fear and Peace
- Surrender and Trust
- God's Sovereignty and Provision

After you choose the topic, read through my personal introduction for each topic and the verses provided. Listen for God's voice—His prompting, leading, direction, conviction, comfort, and encouragement.

Invite the Lord to lead you to a few verses and spend time with them. It might be five or ten minutes. It might be longer. If you have time, read your verse in context with the verses that come before and after it (we talked about this when we learned to memorize our verses and when we spent time in Bible study). Maybe do a Google search, cross-reference (we learned how to do this earlier), or look at the concordance in the back of your Bible for more verses speaking to this topic. Jot down the verses you choose and any other verses you may find.

Within each topic you'll notice I include a "thoughts the Lord brought to mind" section. In this section, I listened for the Holy Spirit to speak as I read through the verses. Please know my heart, friend. I'm not rewriting the verse or passage. I'm not adding to God's Word with these thoughts. They are my words, not God's. They came as I spent time thinking and praying over the passages. My prayer is that these thoughts will help you listen for the Lord's voice as you spend time with Him in His Word.

After you've finished these steps, prayerfully write the prayer God lays on your heart.

FEAR AND PEACE

I shared earlier how a few days after my college graduation, I found an armed, masked man hiding in my apartment. That horrible incident spiraled me into a place of fear and anxiety that held me captive for nearly a decade. Satan used that fear to keep me from living in the fullness and freedom for which God created me. You may find yourself in a similar place. Remember, you're fighting a *spiritual* battle. But it is a battle Jesus has already won! Why? Because by His death and resurrection Jesus conquered sin, fear, and death (2 Timothy 1:10; Hebrews 2:14). As a saved child of God, you and I are His beloved daughters. Because of our identity as God's daughters, we are also conquerors. And not just that; Romans 8:37 tells us we are *more than* conquerors through Christ Jesus!

We have a choice at this point. You either continue to believe the Enemy's lies and remain imprisoned in your fear and anxiety, or you walk fiercely and confidently in the power and work of Jesus to defeat them.

I found verses that directly addressed my fear. I began to pray powerful, earth-shaking, faith-transforming verses. On that particular night, these verses broke the chains of fear that had held me captive for so many years. I fell on my knees before God that night and wept, praising Him for His faithfulness. And I haven't stopped telling my story since! God replaced my fear with trust and peace, the peace that was already mine in Christ Jesus. It is the peace that passes all under-standing. That peace is not of this world; it's found only in Jesus—in His Spirit living in us.

Fear Verses

Have I not commanded you? Be strong and courageous.
Do not be afraid; do not be discouraged, for the LORD your
God will be with you wherever you go. (Joshua 1:9)

So do not fear, for I am with you;
do not be dismayed, for I am your God.
I will strengthen you and help you;
I will uphold you with my righteous
right hand. (Isaiah 41:10)

The LORD is my light and my salvation—
whom shall I fear?
The LORD is the stronghold of my life—
of whom shall I be afraid? (Psalm 27:1)

When I am afraid, I put my trust in you. (Psalm 56:3)

For God gave us a spirit not of fear but of power and
love and self-control. (2 Timothy 1:7 ESV)

You, dear children, are from God and have overcome
them, because the one who is in you is greater than
the one who is in the world. (1 John 4:4)

Thoughts the Lord brought to mind . . .

- Do not be afraid, my child. I'm always with you. I will never leave you. I will help you and hold you in the palm of my hand.
- Fear is not from me. I give you my Holy Spirit, who gives you access to my power, my love, and my mind. My Spirit is stronger than anyone or any circumstances you face. Remember, you are an overcomer because greater is the One who lives in you, which is me, than the one who lives in the world.
- I am your rescuer and defender! I am your stronghold. So, you should fear nothing and no one! I will never leave you nor forsake you. Take refuge in me.

Peace Verses

> In peace I will lie down and sleep,
>> for you alone, LORD,
>> make me dwell in safety. (Psalm 4:8)

> God is our refuge and strength,
>> an ever-present help in trouble. (Psalm 46:1)

> Cast your cares on the LORD
>> and he will sustain you;
> he will never let
>> the righteous be shaken. (Psalm 55:22)

> Whoever dwells in the shelter of the Most High
>> will rest in the shadow of the Almighty.
> I will say of the LORD, "He is my refuge and my fortress,
>> my God, in whom I trust." (Psalm 91:1–2)

Peace is what I leave with you; it is my own peace that I give you. I do not give it as the world does. Do not be worried and upset; do not be afraid. (John 14:27 GNT).

But the Holy Spirit produces this kind of fruit in our lives: love, joy, peace, patience, kindness, goodness, faithfulness, gentleness, and self-control. There is no law against these things! (Galatians 5:22–23 NLT)

Thoughts the Lord brought to mind . . .

- Daughter, cast your cares upon me. Don't you know how much I care for you? I will carry them for you. I will not let you fall. My Spirit, my power, and my love will sustain you. Trust me.
- My Spirit lives in you. The fruit of my Spirit fills you. Peace is part of that fruit. Believe my promise. Walk in my promise. Then you'll live abundantly in my promises.
- I will keep you in perfect peace when you trust in me. You will lie down in peace and rest when you keep your eyes fixed on me. I am your fortress and safe place. Take refuge in me.

SURRENDER AND TRUST

Next, we'll spend time with the words "Surrender" and "Trust." Oh, these are two of the hardest things to do when walking through trials! The Enemy prowls around, waiting for these trials to hit our lives. He initiates his strategy of deception in these trials, telling us that God has abandoned us. Believing those lies causes us to doubt God's goodness and faithfulness. We feel these emotions most often when we're struggling to trust God's timing. At other times we may be confused by

His perceived silence or that the answer we think we've heard doesn't play out. I've walked through each of these waits and am in an especially hard one at the time I write this. One thing I've learned is that if we don't run *to* God, we'll run *away* from God. That running will take us to even lonelier, darker places where we will drift deeper and deeper into uncertainty and doubt.

When we call out these lies and surrender them to God, and when we muster up even a mustard seed of faith and trust, that is when we open a pathway for God to move. It's only through God's Word and His Spirit that we can stand firm against those lying voices of the Enemy planting and spreading seeds of doubt and defeat.

Let's remember what we've learned through our sacred pauses. Even when we can't see, feel, or hear God, He is there! He has promised us in His Word that He will never leave us nor forsake us (Deuteronomy 31:6; Matthew 28:20; Hebrews 13:5). We need to cling to these promises and surrender. Surrender means to yield, relinquish, submit. We need to raise the white flag and loosen our tight grip on what we want, then place it in the hands of our Abba Father, who is more than able to carry the load.

Surrender Verses

> Cast your cares on the LORD
> and he will sustain you;
> he will never let
> the righteous be shaken. (Psalm 55:22)

> Hear my cry, O God;
> listen to my prayer.
>
> From the ends of the earth I call to you,
> I call as my heart grows faint;
> lead me to the rock that is higher than I.

For you have been my refuge,
  a strong tower against the foe.
    (Psalm 61:1–3—David's cry to God)

He heals the brokenhearted
  and binds up their wounds. (Psalm 147:3)

A bruised reed he will not break,
  and a smoldering wick he will not snuff out.
In faithfulness he will bring forth justice;
  he will not falter or be discouraged
till he establishes justice on earth.
  In his teaching the islands will put their hope.
    (Isaiah 42:3–4)

Because of the LORD's great love we are not consumed,
  for his compassions never fail.
They are new every morning;
  great is your faithfulness.
    (Lamentations 3:22–23)

But he said to me, "My grace is sufficient for you, for
my power is made perfect in weakness." Therefore I will
boast all the more gladly about my weaknesses, so that
Christ's power may rest on me. (2 Corinthians 12:9)

Thoughts the Lord brought to mind . . .

- Surrender your broken places to me, my child. They are opportunities for you to experience me in all my fullness and for me to display my glory.
- Always filter your hurt through my unconditional, everlasting, abundant love and compassion. Invite me into your pain. I will bind your wounds. My healing balm will soothe your wounded heart and soul.
- Surrender everything to me. Let it all go. I will carry it. My grace is sufficient for you. My power is made perfect in your weakness.

Trust Verses

> But I trust in you, LORD;
>> I say, "You are my God."
> My times are in your hands;
>> deliver me from the hands of my enemies,
>> from those who pursue me.
> Let your face shine on your servant;
>> save me in your unfailing love.
>> (Psalm 31:14–16)

> He says, "Be still, and know that I am God;
>> I will be exalted among the nations,
>> I will be exalted in the earth."
>> (Psalm 46:10)

> Your word, LORD, is eternal;
>> it stands firm in the heavens.
>> (Psalm 119:89)

Trust in the LORD with all your heart
and lean not on your own understanding;
in all your ways submit to him,
and he will make your paths straight. (Proverbs 3:5–6)

Then Jesus came to them and said, "All authority in heaven
and on earth has been given to me." (Matthew 28:18)

Therefore, there is now no condemnation for those
who are in Christ Jesus. (Romans 8:1)

But if we walk in the light, as he is in the light, we have
fellowship with one another, and the blood of Jesus,
his Son, purifies us from all sin. (1 John 1:7)

Thoughts the Lord brought to mind . . .

- I am all authority in heaven and on earth. No circumstance, person, place, hurt, or sickness is outside my reach or beyond my control. Nothing burdening your heart is too hard for me. Trust me.
- Trust me with your past. No sin is so great that my Son's shed blood will not cover it. Walk out of the darkness and into the light. In me you'll find no condemnation, only grace.
- My Son gave His life for you, revealing my everlasting, lavish love for you. Never doubt that. We settled that on Calvary, when My Son poured out His blood and the veil was torn. So come to me. Trust me with all your heart. Don't lean on your human knowledge and understanding. Submit what you are clinging to into my hands. I will show you the way.

GOD'S SOVEREIGNTY AND PROVISION

I seem to struggle the most with God's sovereignty and provision. I ask and pray for things that seemingly align with God's Word and His good plans for me or my family. I tell Him that if He answers my prayer, He'll get all the glory. I will point others to Him. My child's faith will grow. But then that specific answer never comes. Sometimes what comes is quite the opposite. That's really hard. I find myself getting angry with God. I question His goodness, even though I know I shouldn't. This brings guilt.

In those places, I remind myself where God has been faithful before, whether in my life or in Scripture. I reread my journals and stories from the Bible that reveal God's faithfulness. They redirect my heart and mind to again trust God's sovereignty. They remind me that I can trust His complete control of everything. I can be assured that nothing passes through to me that has not first passed through His hands.

I know that this sovereignty is bathed in love. It's not a hammer. It's not cold and calculating. It's not ruled by harsh decrees. Rather, God's sovereignty flows from a Father's heart consumed by a lavish love for His children. He is a God who promises to give us the desires of our heart **when our desires align with His**.

That is the key. We're on a journey of sanctification—of God working in and through us to mold and shape us to become more like Jesus. So when God withholds that answer or answers it differently, we can trust that He is protecting us. Trust that *Jehovah Jireh*, God our Provider, will provide what's best in His sovereign plan for us.

God's Sovereignty (God Is in Control) Verses

> And these are but the outer fringe of his works;
> how faint the whisper we hear of him!
> Who then can understand the thunder of his power?
> (Job 26:14)

Remember the former things, those of long ago;
    I am God, and there is no other;
    I am God, and there is none like me.
I make known the end from the beginning,
    from ancient times, what is still to come.
I say, "My purpose will stand,
    and I will do all that I please."
        (Isaiah 46:9–10)

"For my thoughts are not your thoughts,
    neither are your ways my ways,"
        declares the LORD.
"As the heavens are higher than the earth,
    so are my ways higher than your ways
    and my thoughts than your thoughts."
        (Isaiah 55:8–9)

When they saw him, they worshiped him; but some doubted.
Then Jesus came to them and said, "All authority in heaven
and on earth has been given to me." (Matthew 28:17–18)

For in him all things were created: things in heaven and
on earth, visible and invisible, whether thrones or powers
or rulers or authorities; all things have been created
through him and for him. He is before all things, and in
him all things hold together. (Colossians 1:16–17)

Thoughts the Lord brought to mind . . .

- Every season has its own beauty—look for it! I am there in your midst. Look for me. Not one thing you're walking through and experiencing is out of my control. I see you.
- Don't miss the wonder of I AM. Of *who* I am. I Am the One True God. There is no one greater or more powerful. Trust me with all that burdens your heart . . . that you can't understand . . . that you feel you cannot bear . . . because I am over it all; I am in it, and I am enough.
- I am completely faithful with each place I walk you through—the valleys and the mountaintops. Trust me with each place, because I'm drawing you closer to me.

God's Provision Verses

So Abraham called that place The LORD Will Provide.
And to this day it is said, "On the mountain of the
LORD it will be provided." (Genesis 22:14)

Let them give thanks to the LORD for his unfailing love
and his wonderful deeds for mankind,
for he satisfies the thirsty
and fills the hungry with good things. (Psalm 107:8–9)

However, as it is written:

"What no eye has seen,
what no ear has heard,
and what no human mind has conceived"—
the things God has prepared for those who love him—

these are the things God has revealed to us by his Spirit.

The Spirit searches all things, even the deep
things of God. (1 Corinthians 2:9–10)

And God is able to bless you abundantly, so that in all
things at all times, having all that you need, you will
abound in every good work. (2 Corinthians 9:8)

Now to him who is able to do immeasurably more than all we
ask or imagine, according to his power that is at work within us,
to him be glory in the church and in Christ Jesus throughout all
generations, for ever and ever! Amen. (Ephesians 3:20–21)

Thoughts the Lord brought to mind . . .

- My beloved daughter, I am *Jehovah Jireh*, your Provider. What I want most is to give you more of me. Delight yourself in me, and I will give you the desires of your heart.
- I am the God of all grace who longs to give you an unlimited supply of my riches. Don't live in scarcity. Don't try to do this on your own. Come to me. Remember that in me, you lack nothing.
- I may provide differently than you've asked. Remember, I see what you cannot perceive. Remember, I have good plans for you. Invest where I have you. Look for how I'm using you. Listen to what you hear. You will be blessed when you do.

☞ **Now, it's your turn to write your prayer. Find a quiet place. Invite God in. Please know, I've already prayed for you as you step into this time of solitude with the Lord. So write with confidence, daughter!**

The Lord is present with you, giving you understanding and leading your study time and prayer.

_____

_____

_____

_____

_____

CLOSING REFLECTIONS

As we close this chapter, I'm sharing a prayer from my journal:

Father, thank You that I am Your beloved daughter. Thank You that I know You are safe and good. As anxiety consumes me, I will stand firm on the Truth I know. You are my refuge and strength, my very present help in trouble (Psalm 46:1). You order my steps. You delight in my way. Though I may fall, and even fail at times, I will not be utterly cast down because You uphold me with Your hand (Psalm 37:23–24). You are for me (Psalm 118:7). When the enemy comes in like a flood and lies overtake me, your Spirit will lift a standard against him and chase him away (Isaiah 59:19).

I will not throw my confidence away because You greatly reward it. Instead, I will persevere so that when I have done Your will, I will receive what You have promised (Hebrews 10:35). I will wait on You, God, even in this hard place. I will have courage because Your Word tells me that in this place You will strengthen me. I will see Your goodness (Psalm 27:13–14).

Give me the manna I need for today. That will be enough to sustain me (Deuteronomy 8:3). I trust that You are always with me. I will not be shaken, for You are right beside me (Psalm 16:8). You are my strength and shield. Thank You for Your promises and that they will *not return void (Isaiah 55:11). I stand on these promises today and wait on You, Lord. And I pray them all in Jesus's name, the author and finisher of my faith. Amen.*

And some closing words on prayer from my friend, Jodie Berndt:

[The] very struggles—the money troubles, the rocky relationships, the substance abuse, the spiritual doubt, and all of the other things that keep us up at night and make us wonder what lies in store for our [. . .] future—are the ties that forever bind our heart to God's.[5]

Friend, thank you for pressing through this chapter. It required hard work and some intense prayer time, maybe more than you're used to. Please don't stop here. Continue your journey of going deeper into prayer. Keep meeting God in His Word. Keep seeking Him for verses and passages to pray. Keep writing prayers.

Also, share your prayers with your friends and family. It's one of the sweetest ways to bless and encourage others in any season.

CLOSING WORDS FROM MY HEART TO YOURS

We started our journey with the cry of my heart: *Lord, please settle my unsettled soul.*

I then asked if you too have an unsettled soul. Do you remember?

This is the unsettledness that overwhelms us as we wonder, *where are You, God? Where are You in my unanswered prayers? In my desperate financial situation? In my chronic pain? In my complicated and exhausting family relationships?*

This unsettledness leads us to ask more questions about God's goodness and character. Is His Word trustworthy? Is His love genuine?

The good news is, we've learned that when we don't understand, when nothing makes sense, or when we don't have the answers we want, we know the One who does. He is the only One who brings true and lasting rest for our soul.

He is the One who is the Ancient of Days (Daniel 7:9–10).

He is the One who was, is, and forever will be (Hebrews 13:8).

He is the One who gave us words about the possible during impossible times. We still need to hear these words today:

> Do not be afraid or discouraged because of this vast army.
> For the battle is not yours, but God's.... You will not have to
> fight this battle. Take up your positions; stand firm and see the
> deliverance the LORD will give you, Judah and Jerusalem. Do not
> be afraid; do not be discouraged. Go out to face them tomorrow,
> and the LORD will be with you." (2 Chronicles 20:15, 17)

After I shared my story of what felt so impossible, I offered you this invitation:

If you want to experience God's deep, abiding rest and walk in the assurance that He sees you, hears you, and loves you, accept this invitation so together we can drink deeply from God's sacred well and allow that living water to settle our unsettled souls.

Now we find ourselves on the other side of that invitation.

We've spent time investigating and discovering answers for our unsettled souls in the holy habits of solitude, silence, and prayer. We've engaged with God in new ways through set-apart pauses in our day. These pauses have allowed us to drink deeply from God's sacred well of living water. Holy habits have provided opportunities for us to redirect our emotions, renew our minds, and refresh our souls.

We've learned that we get to choose. We can live fearfully and anxiously, allowing this fear and anxiety to lead us down rivers of despair and discouragement, or we can slow down, be still, and take sacred pauses with God.

The choice is ours.

It matters *where* we fix our eyes, *on whom* we fix our hope, and *how* we spend our time.

God is our hope . . . our only true hope (Psalm 62:5).

So run to the One who is your strength and your shield (Psalm 28:7). He fights for you (Exodus 14:14). His presence will never leave you. He will never forsake you (Deuteronomy 31:6).

The name of the Lord is a strong tower to which we can run and are safe, even in the worst of life's storms (Proverbs 18:10).

Whether He stills the storm or invites you in, He will be with you, my friend. Of this you can always be certain.

I know you may still wrestle with your unsettled soul. I know I do, and that comforts me. We're not alone.

Remember what I told you at the beginning of our journey? I prayed for every person who would one day read these words. I prayed for you. You were in my heart as I wrote each word. God has forever knit our hearts together through these pages.

God went before you. He led you here. He has walked with you chapter by chapter, page by page, and Scripture by Scripture. My prayer now is that your heart feels a few steps closer to settled. Your soul feels a little more at rest. And I fully trust that God will be faithful to continue the good work He has begun in you.

Yes, the journey we walk this side of heaven is often hard. Yes, sometimes hope can feel so far away that you wonder if it will ever really come. Yes, you don't have all the answers and neither do I. But I trust that God has shifted your mindset because you have the comfort of knowing God's precious presence is right here with you. Always!

Hear these words from my heart to yours. Whatever you're believing God for today, I'm believing it with you—one hundred percent!

El Roi, our God who sees, absolutely sees your tears. He hears your cries. So draw close and hear these whispered words from my heart:

I know this is hard.
> *What you feel is real.*
> *And though God feels far, He is near. Right there with you.*
> *He's working things out for your good.*

And when your prayers aren't answered in your time or in your way, it's my deepest prayer that God has shown you through His Word, His names, His attributes, His very presence, and His power that He is good, His love is secure, and His hope is sure.

That, my friend, is truth your soul may rest in.

Rejoice during the days when your soul feels settled and at rest! Enjoy that place for its answered prayer. Walk confidently in God's peace. And when you feel unsettledness well up within you, don't get discouraged. Don't give in or give up.

Recall, return, and remember. Recall what you've studied and learned. Return to your holy habits. And remember that life is a journey! Don't let your solitude, silence, and prayer stop here. Continue to take your sacred pauses. Drink often from God's sacred well. Remember with each pause that you are sojourning with your Creator, the One in whose image you are created.

He is the Light of the World who chases away the darkness.

He is the Bread of Life who fills your emptiness.

He is the Good Shepherd who provides and protects.

He is the Resurrection and Life who revives and renews.

He is the Way who makes a way when there is no way.

He is the Truth who silences every lie.

He is the Prince of Peace who stills your soul.

God is your Rock (Psalm 18:2). His love is steadfast (Lamentations 3:22–23).

As we close our journey, receive this prayer from my heart to yours (taken, in part, from Psalm 3:2–6):

Thank You, Lord, that You are a shield around Your daughter.
You are her glory, the One who lifts her head high.
Thank You that when she calls out to You, Lord,
You will answer her from Your holy mountain.
When she lies down to sleep,

She will awake again, because You, O Lord, sustain her.
Thank You that she will not fear though tens of thousands
Assail her on every side.
Lord, help her to keep her eyes fixed on You and You alone.

PRAYERS

WENDY'S MORNING PRAYER

Lord, I don't know who or what will cross my path today. But I do know that You are my Rock and my Fortress. You are my Shield and my Strong Tower. Help me to anchor myself to You today. Teach me how to stand strong in You and choose only Your way today. Help me walk by Your Truth and not my feelings.

Help me to embrace anything that comes my way as an opportunity to see You at work and as an opportunity to point others to You.

Thank You that You love me and nothing can ever take that away from me! Even if I fail today and fall short, You whisper Your unconditional love deep into my soul and remind me that Your mercies are new every morning.

That is truly amazing, Lord.

Thank You for meeting with me today and wake me again tomorrow with the same sweet whisper of Your love. I can't wait to meet with You again. I ask all this in the powerful and majestic name of Your Son, Jesus! Amen.

FAITH DECLARATION

Father, I praise You that I am fearfully and wonderfully made. Thank You that I am forgiven and redeemed by the blood of Your Son, Jesus.

Thank You that in and through the power of Your Holy Spirit, I am a new creation. Because of Your grace and mercy, I am Your hand-crafted masterpiece, and You have good and perfect purposes for me. Please grant me wisdom and discernment as I live out the plan You have for my life. Help me to discover who You've created me to be. Expose the lies of the Enemy. Give me eyes to see myself, not in the world's eyes, but in Your eyes. Father, may I know deep in my heart that I am holy, created in Your image, and set apart for Your purpose. Open my eyes to see my true beauty, a beauty that reflects Your heart, Your character, Your strength, and Your dignity. Plant Your truths deep in my heart. Empower me to be an influence on the culture around me. Protect me from being influenced by the lies and temptations of that very same culture. Surround me with godly friends and mentors. Fill me with Your Holy Spirit and bless me all the days of my life. I ask all this in the name of Your Son, Jesus. Amen.

Now, declare these truths over your heart:

I am Loved (1 John 3:1)

I am Forgiven (1 John 1:9)

I am Redeemed (Ephesians 1:7)

I am a New Creation (2 Corinthians 5:17)

I am Holy (Hebrews 10:10)

I am a Temple of the Holy Spirit (1 Corinthians 3:16–17)

I am Made with Purpose (Ephesians 2:10; 1 Peter 4:10)

PRAYER FOR LIVING WATER

Abba Father, Your Word promises that whoever believes in You will have rivers of living water flowing from her heart.

I've given my heart to You. I am Your blood-bought daughter. My name is engraved in the palm of Your hand for all eternity.

I'm thirsty. I long for Your living water to flow in all its fullness through me today and every day that You give me on this earth.

Holy Spirit, fill me afresh right now. Fill me to overflowing with the fullness of Your peace, presence, love, joy, and hope.

Just as You ensure a spring is constantly renewed with fresh water to keep it pure and flowing freely, I ask You to renew me today.

Give me an unquenchable thirst as I sit at Your feet; ignite a passion in me for more of You and more of Your Word. Teach me. Convict me. Minister to me. Encourage and equip me.

I love You, Lord, and ask this all in Jesus's most precious name. Amen.

PRAYER FOR YOUR CALLING

Heavenly Father, I come before You on my knees today in complete surrender. My heart's desire is to live my life to honor and glorify You. You alone are the Author of Life. You alone know the plans You have for me. I long to know those plans and live out those plans . . . to live in the fullness of the purposes for which You have created me and be used by You to shine the light of Your love and life into the broken places and sacred spaces in this hurting world.

Saturate every part of my seeking heart with the fullness of Your Spirit. Wrap Your holy hands around my heart in this moment and never let go.

Give me ears to hear even the faintest of Your whispers. Give me a mind to understand every word You speak. Give me an obedient heart to follow every direction You give. Open my eyes to see the places You are calling me to serve so that I can shine and share Your light and love with those around me. And give me the courage to say yes!

Rid my heart of all that is selfish and rebellious. Eradicate my every fear. And, Lord, if there is anything getting in the way of my obedience, reveal it to me. Give me a heart of humility that will enable me to surrender that place to You and Your plan. I truly long to do Your will. I want to do Your will. Help me loosen my grip on everything I'm holding too tightly. I want to leave this prayer with hands wide open.

I long for Your highest and best. Nothing less. I want that abundant life which You promise. Let nothing in me resist obedience to Your calling and Your leading to share the hope, love, and peace I've found and, most especially, the giftedness You have woven into me.

Meet me. Move me. Change me. Empower me to "take the next step" in complete faith and trust. Help me make my life one long walk of obedience. Let Your love and Your Word shape my life. Break my heart for what breaks Yours. Shine through me in all I do and say, wherever my feet take me. Flood my heart with Your all-consuming love so that I can love You and love others with that same love. Father, may I praise You with every breath I take. Fill me with Your joy unspeakable no matter what my circumstances and emotions may be. Equip and empower me to serve You faithfully and walk worthy of the sacrifice You made that day on Calvary. I ask this in the powerful and mighty name of Jesus Christ, my Lord and Savior. Amen.

PRAYER FOR YOUR FAMILY

Heavenly Father, I lay my family before You today, asking that:

Our love for each other will grow deeper and stronger the longer we walk with You and that it will abound more and more and reflect Your character. Help us be patient and kind, not boastful or proud. Help us always think the best of, and seek the best for, each other (1 Corinthians 13:4–7; Philippians 1:9–11).

You help us live in unity, putting each other's needs before our own. Give us oneness of heart through the beautiful thread of Your Holy Spirit that binds us together in Jesus (John 17:11, 21; Philippians 2:1–5).

We would have the mind of Christ and acknowledge You daily, no matter where we are, together or apart. Help us take every thought captive to Your Word, replacing lies with truth. Despair with joy. Grief with hope. Anxiety with peace. Hate with love. Rudeness with kindness. Disrespect with honor (Proverbs 3:5–6; 1 Corinthians 2:11–16; 2 Corinthians 10:3–5).

We will live each and every day in the fullness of Your Spirit and in the abundant life You promise (Ephesians 5:18; John 10:10).

We will be confident in who and Whose we are, never looking to others for affirmation of our value and worth. We know down to the marrow of our bones that these are found solely in You (Psalm 139:13–16; Ephesians 1:3–4, 7–8).

We would hunger for more of You and more of Your Word. May nothing else satisfy us more than spending quiet time alone with You (Psalm 63:1; Matthew 4:4; John 4:13–14; 7:37).

We would daily take up the armor of God to protect us from the evil one. Keep us alert to Satan's temptations, schemes, and lies. By the power of Your Spirit, enable our hearts to fully submit to You so we can confidently resist the devil by speaking one Word alone . . . One name . . . Jesus (John 8:44; Ephesians 6:10–18; James 4:7).

We would be strong, courageous, and bold in a culture hostile to You. May we never be afraid to share our story and the hope we have in You (Joshua 1:9; 2 Corinthians 5:17–20).

You give us servant hearts to serve the least and the lost. Give us eyes to see the ones who need an encouraging word. Give us ears to hear the stories of those who need a listening ear. Give us patience to love those who drive us crazy. Give us a generous heart to share our blessings with those who have needs much greater than ours (Mark 10:44–45; John 15:12; Galatians 6:2; Hebrews 13:16).

You give us hearts of gratitude. Awaken us each morning with Your joy filling our hearts, no matter what the day may hold. May we anticipate divine encounters with You throughout our day . . . to see where You are at work and join You (Psalm 118:24; Romans 15:13; Colossians 2:7; 1 Thessalonians 5:18).

You develop in us prayerful hearts, ones that seek You in all things and for all things. May our hearts be tender to Your voice and leading, ready to pray wherever and for whoever You ask (Philippians 4:6–7; Ephesians 6:18; 1 Thessalonians 5:16–18).

I lay these requests before You, Lord, and thank You in advance that You will do exceedingly, abundantly above all that I could ever ask or imagine. Amen.

PRAYER FOR A CHILD

Father, I pray (child's name) will know how extravagantly and unconditionally You love her, that You will never leave her nor forsake her, and that You gave Your Son so she could have life forever with You.

Father, I pray she will call upon Your Son, Jesus, and confess Him as Lord and Savior of her life and desire to have a personal relationship with Him.

Father, thank You that You created (child's name) with a specific plan and purpose for his life. Thank You that he is valuable and precious in Your sight. Father, give him the mind of Christ that is his in You and help him to fully know and love who he is in You and this great plan You have for him.

Father, I pray he will treasure Your Word above all else. Give him a hunger to read, learn, and love it and live his life according to it.

Father, I pray (child's name) will honor her body as Your temple and keep herself pure in every way. Instill in her the truth that she is created in Your image, worthy of Your highest and best for her life.

Father, may Your Truth reign supreme in her heart and mind. May she live according to Your Word, not the lies of this world. Daily renew her mind with Truth and keep her thoughts centered on whatever is true, noble, right, pure, lovely, excellent, and worthy of praise.

Father, teach (child's name) to trust You with all his heart, lean not on his own understanding, and in all his ways acknowledge You so that You will direct his path.

Protect him from being a people pleaser. May he stand confidently in who he is in You! Guard his mind so he doesn't throw away his confidence. Please richly reward his steadfast confidence.

Father, plant Your love, Your presence, and Your Word deep within (child's name)'s heart. May Your Word reach into the marrow of her bones and ignite an unquenchable passion. Cause her to love You with all her heart, soul, mind, and strength and let nothing override that passion because when she knows, loves, and lives Your truth, it changes everything.

Father, just as Jesus grew, grow my child in wisdom and stature and favor with You and with man. Grow my child to be a person of character, integrity, honesty, and a good name. Thank You in advance for all You will do in and through my prayers. I ask this in the powerful name of Jesus Christ our Lord! Amen.

PRAYER FOR YOU, MOM

Father, thank You that I am Your beloved daughter. You know me by name. I know that You see me and hear me, but right now it's hard. I'm struggling to be the mom I want to be. I know You gave me this child (these children). They are Your precious gift. I also know You promise to equip those whom You call. So I come to You today trusting that You hear the cry of my heart.

I'm weary and exhausted. But I know from Your Word that You are my burden-bearer. I need You to carry my burdens today. I'm choosing to fix my eyes on You, asking You to restore, refill, and refresh my soul. Oh, Father, fill me with the fullness of Your Spirit who lives and breathes in me.

Your Word promises that You equip those whom You call. I know You've called me to be a mama. I believe this is my God-given assignment. But, honestly, I have overwhelmingly hard days that make me doubt that truth. That's why I'm here sitting at Your feet. This is a hard day. I desperately need You today as my Provider and my Sustainer. Pour down Your manna from heaven. Each time I open Your Word, as I sit at Your feet and meet with You, feed me Your living and active Word. Give me what I need. Daily manna, Lord.

I long to walk in Your peace that You've promised, so I surrender my worries and fears to You. Your Word says to be anxious for nothing and pray about everything. That's what I'm doing now. I trust Your Word that says worry and fear are not from You. You, Lord, have given me the peace that passes all understanding. You have given me a sound mind, the mind of Christ, which is an ordered mind that trusts and believes in You. Give me the strength and courage to walk in that mind and in Your peace.

Lord, awaken me each day with joy—Your joy! Each morning, as I set my feet on the floor, breathe Your breath of life into the depths of my soul. Fill me with Your fruit—fresh fillings of Your love, joy, peace, patience, kindness, goodness, faithfulness, gentleness, and self-control, a perfect portion for what I need that day.

Remind me that I don't do this alone. You are with me . . . always. You are as near as my next breath. I trust You. I love You. Thank You that in You I can do this! I ask all this in Jesus's name, amen.

PRAYER FOR A FATHER

Lord, thank You for the gift of (father's name). Bless and establish the work of his hands. May he be diligent and prosperous in all he does. Fill him daily with wisdom and discernment. Equip him with what he needs for each day. Give him strength to successfully perform every opportunity which You lay before him.

Father, he is Your unique creation, created by Your hand with a plan and purpose which You laid out before time began. Keep his eyes fixed on You. Lead and guide his every step to accomplish that plan. Guard his heart and mind in Christ Jesus. Protect him from temptation.

Lord, thank You that You are gracious and merciful, all-powerful, and understanding. This world can be a challenging and discouraging place. Grant him the strength for every challenge he encounters. By Your Spirit, enable him to be bold and courageous no matter what this world brings.

Thank You for Your Word, for its power, and for Your promise that it will never return void. Guide him as our spiritual leader and provider. Lead his head and his heart in our relationship, our family, his work, his friendships, our church, and our home.

Lord, money yields the greatest potential to cause problems in a home. Give him wisdom as he seeks to honor You with our finances. I praise You for the blessings You've so generously provided, and I pray You would help him and us to always honor You first as we work in budgets and spending.

Give him a pure heart that seeks to love You and trust You with everything he has and is. Protect him from opinions intended to sway him from Your Truth or lead him astray. Keep his speech pure before You.

Bless him with edifying friendships. Bless us with friends who know, love, and honor You in their hearts and homes. May these friends speak life and hope into our lives and hold us accountable.

Thank you for how You've equipped him, Lord. May he walk in the ways of Jesus and model for his children how to be a man of character, integrity, generosity, honesty, and a good name. I ask this all in Jesus's magnificent and powerful name. Amen.

PRAYER FOR WHEN A FRIEND LOSES A CHILD

Abba Father, when I try to understand the loss of a child, it seems senseless, even cruel. It seems troublesome in my sight until I bring it to You . . . till I come into Your sanctuary. Then I remember that nothing comes into our lives that has not first passed through Your hands (Psalm 103:19; 139:1–18).

Father, lead these broken parents consumed by pain, grief, and hurt to You, the One who created their child and loves him more than anyone ever could.

I ask that during this time of deep grief, You supply all their needs according to the riches of Your glory found only in Christ Jesus (Philippians 4:19). Thank You for Your promise that as they draw near to You, You will come near to them (James 4:8). Surround them with Your loving-kindness. Thank You that Your compassions never fail. They are new every morning. Great is Your faithfulness (Lamentations 3:22–24).

Father, thank You that those who wait for You will gain new strength. They will mount up with wings like eagles. They will run and not be tired, they will walk and not grow weary (Isaiah 40:31). We pray these promises, Father . . . for them to walk in Your strength, to be lifted on the wings of Your angels, and to be carried by Your love.

Thank You for Your promise that Your eyes range throughout the earth to strengthen those whose hearts are fully committed to You. Draw close to them now (2 Chronicles 16:9). Minister to them as only You can do.

We stand on this truth for this family: "'For I know the plans I have for you,' declares the LORD, 'plans to prosper you and not to harm you, plans to give you hope and a future. Then you will call on me and come and pray to me, and I will listen to you. You will seek me and find me when you seek me with all your heart'" (Jeremiah 29:11–13).

Their devastating loss seems to make absolutely no sense. It's a life cut short before it's fully lived. But in Your plan, Lord, somehow it does make sense. We cannot see or understand it right now. But I boldly ask that in their sorrow, pain, and grief, as they seek You, may they find You in ways they never have before. And I ask that You uphold them with Your mighty right hand. Let them trust in Your plan even though right now it seems senseless.

Remind them that, although it may not feel like it now, nothing will ever separate them from Your love—neither death nor life, neither angels nor demons, neither things present nor in the future, nor any powers, neither height nor depth, nor anything else in all creation will ever separate them from the love of God that is found in Christ Jesus their Lord (Romans 8:38–39).

Thank You, Father, that the sacrifices of God are a broken spirit; a broken and contrite heart You will not despise (Psalm 51:17). Father, meet them in their brokenness, fill them with love, slowly pick up the pieces, and begin to put them together to make a new thing of beauty, whatever that looks like to You.

Father, give them courage and strength to stand on Your Word: DO NOT BE FRIGHTENED, AND DO NOT BE DISMAYED, FOR THE LORD YOUR GOD IS WITH YOU WHEREVER YOU GO (Joshua 1:9). And, Father, no matter where they are or who they are with, as the grief settles may they see You and experience You. Protect their hearts from well-meaning but hurtful words. Place Your ministering angels around every corner so they know You are with them.

Finally, Father, we take comfort in 2 Corinthians 4:16–18: "Therefore we do not lose heart. Though outwardly we are wasting away, yet inwardly we are being renewed day by day. For our light and momentary troubles are achieving for us an eternal glory that far outweighs them all. So we fix our eyes not on what is seen, but on what is unseen, since what is seen is temporary, but what is unseen is eternal." I ask all this in Jesus's most precious and powerful name. Amen.

PRAYER FOR AN UNSAVED LOVED ONE

Heavenly Father, you know that my heart breaks for my unsaved loved one [name]. How I long for her to know Your unconditional, deep, and abiding love. I long for her to know Jesus as her Lord and Savior and experience the freedom that comes with His lavish love.

I also know that Your Word says no one can come to Jesus unless You first draw him. So I ask you to draw my loved one [name] close. Open his heart to receive the gospel. Call him by name, even though he doesn't acknowledge or believe in You. Help him to know that You planned every day of his life before he took a single breath. You knew his name. You formed and shaped him.

Lead her heart to the truth of who You are and how lost she is without You. Free her from the lies of this culture and the schemes of the evil one who deceives her by telling her that You are not real, are not significant, and are not the way to salvation, freedom, hope, and healing. Demolish every lie she believes that sets itself up against truth.

Open his eyes to turn from darkness to light and from death to life. Move him to experience godly sorrow that brings repentance. Move his heart to believe and understand that he needs forgiveness and give him the desire to receive it. Remove his hardened heart and replace it with a heart of flesh willing to receive truth and be transformed by it.

Put Your Spirit in her. Touch her in real and personal ways so that she will know that she has received You. Give her understanding as she opens her Bible. Move her to follow You with her whole heart and obey Your words.

Create in him a pure heart. Renew a steadfast spirit in him. Instill in him the joy of his salvation. Have compassion on him as he walks this journey. Be patient and kind, and gracious and merciful. Cause him to hear Your voice when he begins to doubt and wander. Lead him with kindness back to You.

Father, help me pray with open hands, trusting You and You alone. Keep me from manipulating or trying to make this happen in my own strength. On this journey, help me be joyful in hope, patient in affliction, and faithful in prayer. I stand firm believing that You have begun a good work in her heart, and You will complete it. I stand firm believing that one day I will celebrate that though she was once lost, she will be found. She will be a beloved child of the One True God. I ask this in Jesus's name, amen.

PRAYING ON THE ARMOR OF GOD

Father, strengthen (name) with Your Helmet of Salvation. He's been bought at a high price: Your Son's precious blood. He's a saved child of God. You've given him the mind of Christ so that he can STAND firm against Satan's schemes and lies.

Father, thank You that his heart is covered with the Breastplate of Righteousness. Thank You that Jesus defeated the power of sin and death at the cross and it no longer has dominion over him. You've forgiven him of his sin and clothed him with Your righteousness. He STANDS firm in that righteousness!

Father, gird him with the Belt of Truth. We know and believe that Your Word is truth. It's that truth, and that truth alone, which sets him free. He has chosen to believe Your truth above all else, rejecting every lie of the evil one. He STANDS firm against the antichrist spirit and his temptations, deceptions, schemes, and accusations!

Father, shod his feet with the Shoes of the Gospel of Peace. Make him ready to march into any battle set before him. Fill him with Your peace. He chooses to be an instrument of Your peace, to always forgive and not harbor bitterness and anger. He STANDS ready to live out and give an account for the faith he has in You today.

Father, he holds up the Shield of Faith. He trusts and believes You at Your Word that You are the King of Kings, the Lord of Lords, and the Great I AM. You alone are the Author and Perfecter of his faith. He trusts You to meet all his needs. He rejects a spirit of fear and STANDS firm in the spirit of Your power, love, and a sound mind!

Finally, he takes up the Sword of the Spirit. He loads his arsenal with Your rhema words given directly from Your heart to his. He chooses to hide Your Word in his heart and to speak it boldly as led by Your Spirit. He chooses to believe Your truth over Satan's lies. Pour out Your Truth and Your Spirit over his life. Fill him with all wisdom and understanding. He chooses this day to STAND firm on Your living and active Word.

Father, thank You for Your mighty weapons. Thank You that You have already won this battle. Thank You that he is a victor and that greater are You who lives in him than he who lives in this world. Thank You that he can do all things through Your Son, Jesus, who strengthens him. He surrenders his battles to You and comes under Your power and Your authority. Fill him with the fullness of Your Spirit.

We have prayed according to Your Word, and You've said that You watch over Your Word to perform it. We stand on that today. We ask this all in Jesus's name, amen.

PRAYER FOR SENDING A CHILD TO COLLEGE

Heavenly Father, thank You for (name). You created her and knit her together in the secret place. You knew her name before she took a single breath. You have called her as Your own, and now she steps out in faith to follow where You lead.

As she leaves home and embarks on the next journey You have planned for her, keep Your hand upon her. May she find favor, good standing, and high esteem in Your eyes and in the eyes of her professors, administrators, classmates, and friends. Grant her great wisdom and understanding as she moves into this next phase of her education. May this wisdom be Yours and Yours alone. Give her a spirit of discernment to recognize lies from truth. Fill her with knowledge and understanding as she reads and studies for each class.

Keep her ever mindful that You are the source of all wisdom and knowledge no matter what anyone else says. You are the Alpha and the Omega, the Beginning and the End, the First and the Last. As she learns and grows in wisdom and knowledge, may she bear fruit in every good work. Bless and establish the work of her hands.

Father, keep Your hand of protection upon her. Surround her with your angels. May she forever dwell under the shadow of Your wing. When things get tough, or when she feels lonely or fearful, remind her that You are her refuge and her strength. May she know deep in her heart that You will never leave her nor forsake her. Be a shield about her. Preserve her in all her ways.

Bring across her path godly men and women of integrity and strong character. May they model a life that pleases You and influence her in ways that will draw her closer to You and not further away.

Father, keep her pure as the world presses in with temptations, lies, and deceit. Give her the mind of Christ. Enable her to take every thought captive to the obedience of Christ. Give her the courage to say no and to go her own way and not the way of others. As she humbles herself in this way, I pray that You will elevate her in their eyes and lift her up!

Father, continue to grow her faith deeper year after year. Lead her to a church home where she can worship You and learn more about You, a Bible study where she can study Your Word, and a fellowship of believers she can lean on for prayer and support. Keep her strong in You and allow her to be salt and light. May her life shine Your love, and may she draw others closer to You by how she lives her life.

Thank You that You are faithful to Your Word and will do what I ask when I ask what is in Your will and in Your name. I ask all this in Jesus's name, amen.

PRAYING THROUGH THE TABERNACLE

Sanctifying (Exodus 27:1–8; Romans 12:1)

Father, just as the priest came before You at the brazen altar, I come before You today, offering myself as a living sacrifice, holding nothing back. Ignite a fire in my heart and keep it ever burning with a passion for more of You. With every fiber of my being, help me to comprehend deep in my soul how wide and long and high and deep is Your great love for me. As that love consumes me, help me to love You back with abandon, desiring You above all else this world offers. Empower me to die to self and envelop my will in Your will.

Cleansing (Exodus 30:17-21; Romans 12:2; Hebrews 4:12)

Father, just as the priest washed himself in the laver, wash me with Your Word. Cleanse my heart and renew my mind. As I look into Your living, active, life-transforming Word, give me eyes to see myself as I really am. Rebuke me. Teach me. Mold me. Convict me. Lead me to repentance. By Your love and grace, transform and restore me. Equip me to live and walk in step with Your Spirit and Your Word.

Filling (Exodus 25:31-40; John 8:12; Ephesians 5:13-20; 1 John 1:5)

Father, just as the priest stood before the lampstand in the Holy Place, I also pause there. I know there is no light apart from You, Lord. Thank You that no matter how dark it might get, You are brighter still. In You, there is no darkness at all! You are the Light of my life and in my life. Lead me, Lord, in the way everlasting. As the oil filled the almond blossoms, fill me when I meet with You. Refresh and renew my spirit. Fix my eyes on You alone. Fill me to overflowing so I can then pour into others.

Strengthening (Exodus 25:23-30; Jeremiah 15:16; John 6:35, 51)

Father, as the priest shared in the bread of the Presence in the Holy Place, I want to feast on You because You alone can satisfy my every need. You are the Bread of Life, and You alone are enough. Strengthen me from within as I feast on Your Word. May I not just ingest but help me to digest each and every morsel. Give me a grateful heart, one sustained by You and You alone, no matter what swirls about me. You are the Bread of Heaven that nourishes, sustains, and strengthens. Jesus, I cannot live without You!

Interceding (Exodus 30:1-10, 34-38; Psalm 141:2; Revelation 5:8)

Father, just as the priest offered incense at the altar of incense, I come before You, offering my prayers. I love that the incense offered in the golden bowls was a pleasing aroma to You. May my prayers be the same. Father, prick my heart to stand in the gap for the broken, the lost, the hopeless, and those in need around me. Give me eyes to see them and a heart of compassion to pray for them. Give me discernment to know for whom and when to pray. Fill my mouth with Your words so that my prayers will be powerful and effective. Thank You that when I pray, the eternal pierces the temporal. Use me in that precious and holy place so I can see Your hand at work in unmistakable and indescribable ways! Break strongholds. Loose chains. Untangle lies. Destroy doubts. Increase faith. Bring salvation. I'm enlisting as a soldier in Your army, Lord. Use me.

Thanksgiving (Exodus 26:31–35; Matthew 27:51; Hebrews 10:19–22)

Thank You, Father, that the veil has been torn and I have this privilege to be in Your presence as the high priest was with You in the Most Holy Place. When I come boldly before You and lift my prayers, You listen! You care. My prayers are a sweet aroma to You. Gratitude fills my heart that You, the God of the universe and the Creator of all things, rejoice over me, delight in me, and desire to meet with me. You know the cry of my heart. Hold me close, Lord. Keep my heart pure. Ready me for that day, that glorious day when I shall stand before You in heaven and see You face to face. Oh, what a joyous day that will be! I will kneel at Your feet and worship You forever.

I love You, Lord, and ask all this in Jesus's magnificent and powerful name. Amen.

PRAYERS FOR YOUR EVERY NEED

Prayer for Your Study Time

Father, thank You for this treasured time to spend with You in Your Word. Help me not to be intimidated or afraid. I trust that You have wonderful things to reveal to me and teach me about You and about myself. Meet with me each time I open Your Word. Help me surrender my heart and mind to You. I want to learn from You and about You. Hide Your truths and promises deep in my soul. Teach me. Move me. Change me. May I never be the same because of the time I spend with You. I pray this in Jesus's name. May all glory, majesty, power, and authority be Yours, now and forevermore. Amen.

Prayer of Personal Declaration

*Through the blood of Jesus, I am **redeemed** out of the hand of the devil.*

*Through the blood of Jesus, my sins are **forgiven**, washed white as snow.*

*Through the blood of Jesus, I am **justified**, made righteous in God's eyes, just as if I'd never sinned.*

*Through the blood of Jesus, I am made **holy** in God's sight, set apart for His purposes.*

*Through the blood of Jesus, I receive the gift of, and am **sealed** by, the Holy Spirit, making my body a living, breathing temple of God's Holy Spirit.*

*Through the blood of Jesus and the indwelling power of His Holy Spirit, I am an **overcomer**. Satan has no hold on me. He has no power over me. He must flee at the name of Jesus.*

Prayer for Another in Need

For Zion's sake I will not keep silent,
for Jerusalem's sake I will not remain quiet,
till her vindication shines out like the dawn,
her salvation like a blazing torch.
The nations will see your vindication,
and all kings your glory;
you will be called by a new name
that the mouth of the LORD will bestow.

You will be a crown of splendor in the LORD's hand,
    a royal diadem in the hand of your God.
No longer will they call you Deserted,
    or name your land Desolate.
But you will be called Hephzibah,
    and your land Beulah;
for the LORD will take delight in you,
    and your land will be married. (Isaiah 62:1–4)

Prayer for the New Year

Father, You are the King of Kings and Lord of Lords, the Sovereign over all things. You know each heart drawn here today. You planned to meet her here in the pages of Your Word. You created her heart and know her every need, deepest desires, scars, and open wounds. Lord, I ask that in this New Year You would fall afresh on her as she prays this prayer:

Father, You are Holy and call Your children to be holy. Yet I confess that so often my heart wanders far from You. My speech does not glorify You, and my actions do not honor You. Tender my heart to receive the words which Your sweet Spirit has for me. Clothe me with humility. Take away my desire to always be right and have my own way. Help me to seek You first in all I say and do. Help me submit to Your Word and allow it to penetrate those deep places in my heart that resist change. If necessary, put me through the refiner's fire to burn off those character traits that keep me from walking in step with You.

Father, give me a heart that loves and seeks after Truth above all else. Give me wisdom and discernment to reject the lies of this world and recognize the schemes of the evil one. Guide me into all Truth. Guard my heart and keep my eyes fixed on You. Fill me with the fruit of your Spirit to make me more like You. As I open Your Word, fill me and saturate me with the fullness of Your holy presence.

Father, today I surrender my thoughts, my speech, and my heart. Thank You that You are Faithful and True. I trust You to do a mighty work in and through me this year. Thank You that what You begin, You will carry on to completion until the day I step into eternity with You. Help me to trust in You with all my heart and lean not on my own understanding. Help me to acknowledge You in all my ways so that I can obey when I hear, "This is the way, walk in it."

Father, I love You and thank You that You love me. May my life be a living testimony of You. I ask this in the powerful and mighty name of Your Son, Jesus Christ our Lord, who will do exceedingly and abundantly above all that I could ever ask or imagine. Amen.

Prayer When You Feel Overwhelmed

Father, today I come to You feeling overwhelmed. Powerless. Weak. I feel as if I can't breathe, and like I can't take that next step. I want to curl up and hide from the world. But, Father, I know those are lies. So, in full confidence, I come to You, the Commander of Heaven's Armies, knowing who You are and whose I am. I am Your lavishly loved blood-bought daughter.

In my weakness, You are strong. In my fear, You are brave. In my anxiety, You are peace. In my sadness, You are joy. In my despair, You are hope.

Today, I remember Your faithfulness—the last time You walked me through a hard place. You used it to mold, prune, and train me. Through it You ensured that I depended upon You and You alone. You used it for my good and Your glory. Keep that memory ever before me. I want to trust You here again, because I know You are for me.

Commander of Heaven's Armies, my battle is YOUR battle to fight. I know You are on my side. I trust You for victory. Empower me to walk through this trial in Your strength and power. I ask this in Jesus's mighty and powerful name, amen.

Prayer for Peace

Heavenly Father, I come before You, the God of Peace, and ask for an extraordinary filling of Your perfect peace—the peace that passes all understanding—to blanket my heart and mind. Father, I know I have the mind of Christ; it is mine in You. So I claim that mind today.

When I choose to shift my focus from You to my calendar and my circumstances, turn my face back to You. Draw me into a sacred pause and meet me there. Still my heart. Settle my soul.

Direct me to Your Word or a song or grant me a sweet nudging from Your Spirit. Keep me focused only on that which is excellent, lovely, and praiseworthy. When anxieties rise within me, lead me by still waters, quiet my heart, and refresh my soul. I know the peace that passes all understanding is mine in Jesus. I believe it; now help me with my unbelief. I love You, Father, and thank You in advance for the precious peace that will fill me each day.

Prayer to Renew Your Walk with God

Heavenly Father, I humbly come before You, seeking a rich abiding relationship with You. I desire above all else to be one with You, attached to Your vine, filled with Your Spirit. I want to live out the plan You have for me . . . the one You laid out before time began. I'm desperate to be the godly woman You're calling me to be.

Soften my heart to receive Your sweet Spirit in all His fullness so that I can reflect Your Spirit in all I say and do. You said that if anyone lacks wisdom, she need only ask for it and You will give it liberally. I'm asking You now. Father, fill me to overflowing with wisdom. Grant me insight and apply my heart to understanding. As I open Your Word, penetrate the deepest places in my heart, especially the places that I don't let anyone in.

Father, may Your peace, not the world's peace—the peace that passes all understanding—guard my heart and rule my life. Give me the desire to meet with You and sit quietly at Your feet.

Father, draw me close. As Your Word fills me, change me from the inside out. Change my heart so that my will may not be done but Yours be done in and through my prayers and my life. Fill me up with the fullness of Your Spirit so that I may accomplish all that I'm asking, for I know that I can't do it in my own strength. I know that I can do this, and all that You call me to, through Christ who strengthens me.

Father, thank You for watching over Your Word to perform it. Thank You that it will accomplish what You desire and achieve the purposes for which You sent it. Beginning today, I will pray Your Word, believing it and Your promises, with all my heart. I thank You in advance for all You will do for me as I walk in obedience to Your command to abide in You. I know that according to Your Word, You will do even more than I could ever ask or imagine in answer to this simple prayer, and I boldly ask this in the powerful name of Jesus Christ my Savior. Amen.

Prayer for Hope and Healing

Heavenly Father, You, and You alone, are my Creator, Redeemer, and the Author and Perfecter of my faith. You alone are Almighty God, the King of Kings and Lord of Lords.

Father, someone broke my heart. It feels crushed beyond repair. I feel helpless and alone, like I'll never feel hope and joy again. I have lived for so long shrouded in despair and darkness. Your Word says that You see me, but it doesn't feel like it. It says You know my every thought, but my reality feels like you don't care. You are so quiet.

I'm trusting that You do see me and hear me because Your Word says You are El Roi, the God who sees Your children.

Father, I come before Your throne of grace and surrender my heart and mind to You. I know Satan schemes to keep me obsessing over my negative thoughts. So today I stand on the truth that I am Your daughter and I have the mind of Christ. Help me to take the lies I'm believing captive with these truths and promises I found in Your Word.

I am . . .

Created in Your Image
Valued and Lavishly Loved
Holy and Set Apart

Molded and Shaped by Your Hand for a Specific Purpose

And, most of all, Lord,
    I BELONG TO YOU!
    I run to You, Father, because You alone are Faithful and True.
    Remind me how valuable I am in Your eyes . . . that You bought me with a price, the shed blood of Your Son, Jesus. Because of this, I am Your child, sealed by Your Spirit for eternity. Father, enable me to stand in that shed blood and walk confidently forward in the power of Your Spirit . . . every footstep leaving a red stain to remind me that I'm not walking alone.
    In Your strength and power, I will walk confidently in my identity as a blood-bought daughter of the One True God. You alone are my Deliverer. My Shield. My Strength. My Rock.
    God, Your Word says that what is impossible with man is possible with You. So, right now, I fully trust in You and that You will heal my heart. And, in the wait, I trust You and know I can do ALL things through You who strengthens me!
    I ask this in the name of Jesus, believing with all my heart that You will be faithful to bring it to pass. Amen.

Prayer to Forgive Someone

Father, thank You for exchanging Your life for mine at the cross and forgiving my sin. Thank You that because of that great exchange and Your resurrection from the dead, Your Spirit now lives in me, empowering me to do what seems impossible in my own strength. Enable and empower me to forgive as You have forgiven me.
    Help me forgive _____. In my own strength, I can't do this. But I trust in Your promise that says I can do all things through Your Son, Jesus, who strengthens me.
    Give me eyes to see _____ the way You see him/her. Take my eyes off my own pain and hurt and keep them fixed on You and You alone. I pray for healing in his/her life as I pray for the

same in mine. Help me surrender all thoughts of judgment, retaliation, punishment, and justice to You. You alone are the Judge. Help me trust in You and You alone to make things right.

Help me speak these words of forgiveness as I sit before You now:
_____, *I forgive you. I forgive every hurt you've committed against me. [Be specific. For example: "I forgive you for not giving me the love and acceptance I desire . . . for abusing me . . . for abandoning me . . . for lying to me . . . for not asking forgiveness for how you've hurt me . . . for not giving me what only Jesus can and should give . . . for how you've betrayed me."] I will no longer expect from you that which you cannot give or provide. I will no longer demand from you what you are incapable of giving. I will look to God and God alone to provide for my every need. In that forgiveness, I gain freedom. I will no longer allow you to hurt me. I will no longer give you power over my life.*

Father, thank You for hearing my prayer and for enabling me to fully forgive _____. *Thank You that I'm no longer bound up in unforgiveness and am now free to be Your vessel and live the abundant life You have planned for me. And when those feelings of unforgiveness slip back in, bring me back to this prayer. I ask all this in Jesus's powerful, life-giving name, amen.*

Prayer for a Sick Friend

Precious Father, I call upon You today as Jehovah Rapha, God our Healer. I stand before You as one undeserving to have You hear my prayers, yet through the gift of Your Son, Jesus, I know I have the right and privilege to come before You. Thank You for that privilege. Thank You that Your Word promises that the prayer of the righteous is powerful and effective. I stand on that promise as I pray for my friend.

I stand boldly and confidently in Your Word as it speaks to healing. Your Word says that a prayer, offered in faith for the sick, will make them well. Your Word says that when Your Son died on the cross, He took our infirmities and bore our sicknesses. Therefore, I stand on the authority of Your written Word which You promise will not return void but accomplish what it says it will, the Word that promises You will do immeasurably more than I could ever ask or imagine through the power of the Holy Spirit that lives within me. Based on this Word, and the blood of Your Son, Jesus, thank You that my friend will be redeemed from her sickness. I pray that every medical treatment will be effective and perfectly accomplish the purposes for which it is given.

In the powerful and mighty name of Jesus I stand against Satan, who tries to operate against those who believe in You and in Your Word. Father, I demolish arguments and every pretension that sets itself up against the knowledge of God and pray that You will take every negative, fearful, doubting thought captive and make it obedient to Christ. I pray against the spirit of fear because Your Word says that as believers we do not have a Spirit of fear but of power, love, and a sound mind. I claim the mind of Christ for my friend. I pray for faith where faith feels impossible. Father, I pray that whatever she has learned or received or heard from You would be put into practice. I pray that she would draw from the deepest places in her heart to combat the lies of the evil one. I place her under the shadow of the Almighty, in the secret dwelling place of the Most High God, where no foe can abide.

Thank You that Your Word abides in her and that the power of Your Holy Spirit resides in her body, the same power that resurrected Jesus from the dead. It is Your Word and this power that will deliver her to wholeness in body and spirit to the very deepest parts of her body, even to her joints and the marrow of her bones and her blood. I stand in the truth that Your Word is medication and life to her flesh. I pray the whole armor of God upon her so that the Sword of the Spirit and the Shield of Faith will now protect her from the evil one, who wants to keep doubt, sickness, and despair in her life.

Until the time Your perfect healing is revealed, Father, I ask You to keep her in perfect peace as she holds her heart steadfast because she trusts in You. Thank You that You will never leave her nor forsake her and that You are at work during even her darkest times, working and willing Your perfect plan. In the still of the night, may she sense Your everlasting peace and presence, Father. May she feel Your loving hand upon her and Your comforting arms around her. When her pillow is wet with tears, Father, may she trust You at Your Word that You see and remember every one of her tears. You know her hurts, doubts, and questions. Father, reveal Yourself to her every moment in real and tangible ways.

I stand immovable and fixed in full assurance that You will show Yourself strong on her behalf and that You will accomplish the health and healing promised in Your Word. I remember that faith is being sure of what we hope for and certain of what we do not see. Thank You in advance for the mighty work You will accomplish in the name of Your Son, Jesus Christ. I ask all these things in the powerful and saving name of Jesus. Amen.

Prayer for When Evil Presses In

Abba Father, day after day horrific events flash before my eyes. Evil people. Angry people. Lost people. Killing. Stealing. Destroying. Hate-filled crimes rock our world. They shake me to the very core. Why, Lord, why? What is going on? Where are You?

My heart aches. It aches for those who have lost daughters, sons, mothers, fathers, sisters, brothers, grandparents, friends, or coworkers. They will never again hear "I love you," never again hold a hand, never again receive a goodnight kiss, never again celebrate a birthday, and never again share an anniversary.

Will this evil come near me? Near my loved ones? I don't want to be afraid, but it's hard. I don't want to worry, but it's getting closer. So, today, I turn my face to You . . . my Hope . . . Shield . . . Defender . . . Strong Tower . . . the One who is Sovereign over everything.

Even when it seems everything around me is falling apart, You hold all things together. You alone are the ruler of heaven and earth, of all the kingdoms of the nations. Power and might are in Your hand. Nothing and no one can stand against You. No purpose of Yours can be thwarted. Remind me of these truths. Enable me by the power of Your Holy Spirit to take every thought captive, Lord. Give me right thinking. Give me the words to speak and the time to speak them. And when it's time to be quiet, lead me to pray.

When fear rises within me, help me press into Jesus, my Redeemer and Savior. He is the One who is the hope of heaven and my hope. In Him I have hope for today, tomorrow, and even to the end of time. Yes, even to the promised marvelous, glorious end of time. It is the time when Jesus, King of Kings and Lord of Lords, will be crowned Lord of All. It is the time when every knee will bow and every tongue will confess Jesus is Lord.

So, although today I weep and grieve, I won't give in to despair and hopelessness because I stand on solid ground—on the Rock of Ages, Jesus Christ. I stand heart to heart, hand in hand with believers from across the globe proclaiming TRUTH. We declare that Jesus is Lord overall and He is the Destroyer of all evil. He has already overcome the evil one. And because I am in Him, I too am an overcomer!

I stand on the truths from Your living and active Word, God. These words do not return void but will accomplish what You desire and achieve the purposes for which You sent them.

Be strong and courageous. Do not be afraid or terrified because of them, for the LORD your God goes with you; he will never leave you nor forsake you. (Deuteronomy 31:6)

And we know that in all things God works for the good of those who love him, who have been called according to his purpose. (Romans 8:28)

The one who does what is sinful is of the devil, because the devil has been sinning from the beginning. The reason the Son of God appeared was to destroy the devil's work. (1 John 3:8)

You are from God, little children, and have overcome them; because greater is He who is in you than he who is in the world. (1 John 4:4 NASB)

Oh, Father, thank You that even in the face of the most horrific evil, I will walk in absolute victory. I have complete and total confidence that I am and always will be an overcomer by the power of You, my Living God. El Shaddai. Almighty God. The Lord of Hosts. The Commander of Heaven's Armies.

I pray this in the powerful and effective name of Jesus. Amen.

MEMORY VERSES

Psalm 16:8

Isaiah 26:3

Colossians 3:12–13

Hebrews 1:3

Romans 12:10

Romans 15:4

Galatians 5:22–23

Deuteronomy 31:8

Psalm 4:8

2 Timothy 3:16–17

2 Corinthians 12:9

Isaiah 40:31

Psalm 100:4–5

TIPS TO HELP MEMORIZE SCRIPTURE

- **Write the full verse.** Use a notebook, notecards, or a journal.
- **Learn your verse phrase by phrase.**
- **Recite your first phrase until you have it comfortably hidden in your heart.** Move to your next phrase and recite it, always saying the earlier phrases with it.
- **Continue to write your phrase several (3–5) days during the week.** Write in a notebook, on notecards, or in a journal.
- **Circle the words you can't remember.**
- **When you memorize more than one Scripture, keep practicing.** At least 2–3 times a week, write and recite the prior weeks' memory verses before you write/recite your verse for the current week.
- **Incorporate your verse into your prayers.** Talk to God about your verse in prayer. Ask Him to help you learn *and* retain it. Pray and personalize your verse. You may have to change a few words to personalize it.
- **Gain context to your verse.** This means read the sentences and/or passages before and after your verse. Consider why certain words or

the verse itself were included. This gains greater insight into what the verse means.

- **Read the verse in other translations.** Take notes about what you've learned in your notebook or journal or include it on your notecard for that verse.

STEPS FOR SPENDING TIME ALONE WITH GOD

Step One: Invite God in.

Step Two: Start small.

Step Three: Add one minute of stillness and silence.

Step Four: Add another minute or two of silence.

Step Five: Remember that being still is a gift that keeps on giving.

Step Six: Journal what you experience.

RECIPES

CINNAMON BREAKFAST CAKE

Ingredients
- 1 box yellow cake mix
- 1 package instant vanilla pudding
- 2 eggs
- $1/8$ teaspoon vanilla
- $1^1/_4$ cups water
- $1/2$ cup oil
- $1/2$ cup mixture of sugar and cinnamon

Mixing Instructions
For best results, use an electric mixer

Add cake mix and pudding to a large mixing bowl.

Add eggs, vanilla, water, and oil to the large bowl.

Mix ingredients together on medium speed for 4–5 minutes (this is what makes it fluffy!).

Baking Instructions
Grease a 9x13-inch pan.

Pour $1/2$ of the batter into the pan and sprinkle $1/2$ of the cinnamon/sugar mixture over that layer.

Pour the remaining batter into the pan and sprinkle the remaining cinnamon/sugar mixture over that layer.

Swirl the batter using a knife.

Bake at 350 degrees for approximately 45 minutes (check with a toothpick at about 35–40 minutes; it's done when the toothpick comes up clean).

The cake should be light and fluffy.

Enjoy!

> In the morning, LORD, you hear my voice;
> in the morning I lay my requests before you
> and wait expectantly. (Psalm 5:3)

HOMEMADE COCONUT GRANOLA

Ingredients

One (7-ounce) package UNSWEETENED coconut flakes

Chopped nuts (1 to 2 handfuls of almonds and chopped pecans mixed together, 1 handful of pumpkin seeds and sunflower seeds mixed together, and 1 to 2 tablespoons chia seeds. You can add any other nuts you like)

$1/4$ cup coconut oil

$1/4$ cup maple syrup OR honey OR agave or combine a few of them

1 teaspoon vanilla

Mixing Instructions

Combine coconut and nuts in a large bowl.

In a small saucepan over medium heat, bring coconut oil and syrup to a boil (watch carefully—it comes to a boil quickly).

Add vanilla to this mixture while it's boiling and stir.

Add hot mixture to coconut/nut mixture and toss until the nuts
are completely coated.

Spread evenly on a cookie sheet and lightly pat down (I place a
sheet of parchment paper on the cookie sheet first to avoid
sticking).

Baking Instructions

Bake for 10 minutes. If the granola needs more browning, add 2
more minutes at a time and watch CAREFULLY because it
will burn quickly.

Cool and enjoy!

Then Jesus declared, "I am the bread of life. Whoever
comes to me will never go hungry, and whoever
believes in me will never be thirsty." (John 6:35)

RECOMMENDED RESOURCES LIST

STUDY BIBLES

Barker, Kenneth L., Mark L. Strauss, Jeannine K. Brown, Craig L.
    Blomberg, and Michael Williams, eds. *NIV Study Bible.* Grand
    Rapids, MI: Zondervan, 2020. ISBN: 9780310448945.
ESV Study Bible. Wheaton, IL: Crossway, 2006. ISBN: 9781433502415.
CSB Study Bible. Nashville, TN: Holman Bible Publishers, 2017. ISBN:
    9781433648090.

CONCORDANCES

Strong, James. *The New Strong's Exhaustive Concordance of the Bible.*
    Nashville, TN: Thomas Nelson, 2010. ISBN: 9781418541699.
Kohlenberger, John R., III. *NIV Exhaustive Bible Concordance.* 3rd ed.
    Grand Rapids, MI: Zondervan, 2015. ISBN: 9780310262930.

COMMENTARIES

MacDonald, William. *Believer's Bible Commentary*. 2nd ed., edited
by Art Farstad. Nashville, TN: Thomas Nelson, 2016. ISBN:
9780718076856.

Sailhamer, John H. *NIV Bible Study Commentary*. Grand Rapids, MI:
Zondervan, 2011. ISBN: 9780310331193.

NOTES

INTRODUCTION: Lord, What's Wrong with Me?

1. "Americans Say They Are More Anxious," American Psychiatric Association, May 6, 2018, https://www.psychiatry.org/News-room/News -Releases/Americans-Say-They-are-More-Anxious-Baby-Boomers/.
2. Justin Whitmel Earley, "Unlock the Power of Family Habits," The Gospel Coalition, December 30, 2021, https://www.thegospelcoalition.org /article/unlock-power-family-habits/.

CHAPTER ONE: Lord, Renew My Mind

1. A. W. Tozer, *The Pursuit of God* (Chicago: Moody, 2015), 15.
2. *Merriam-Webster's Collegiate Dictionary*, s.v. "Malleability," last modified April 7, 2023, https://www.merriam-webster.com/dictionary/malleability/.
3. Kendra Cherry, "What Is Neuroplasticity?," Very Well Mind, November 2, 2022, https://www.verywellmind.com/what-is-brain -plasticity-2794886/.
4. "Neuroplasticity," Emotiv, accessed April 21, 2023, https://www.emotiv .com/glossary/neuroplasticity/.
5. Henri Nouwen, *The Way of the Heart: Desert Spirituality and Contemporary Ministry* (San Francisco: HarperOne, 1991), 27–28. The citation comes from Dave Sandel, "The Way of the Heart by Henri Nouwen," *davesandel* (blog), August 27, 2011, https://davesandel.wordpress.com/2011/08/27 /the-way-of-the-heart-by-henri-nouwen/.
6. Henri Nouwen, "Holy Silence," *Daily Meditations* (blog), Henri Nouwen Society, November 24, 2022, https://henrinouwen.org/meditations/holy -silence/.

7. C. H. Spurgeon, "The Truly Blessed Man," Sermon No. 3270, October 5, 1911, https://www.spurgeongems.org/sermon/chs3270.pdf, p. 5.

CHAPTER TWO: Lord, Quiet My Heart

1. John Piper, "Lord, Teach Us to Fight: The Double Battle in Gethsemane," transcript of speech delivered at the London Men's Convention, June 2, 2018, https://www.desiringgod.org/messages/lord-teach-us-to-fight/.

CHAPTER THREE: Lord, Teach Me Your Word

1. David Mathis, "Not One of God's Words Will Fail," Desiring God, August 19, 2019, https://www.desiringgod.org/articles/not-one-of-gods-words-will-fail/.

2. David Guzik, "Study Guide for Genesis Chapter 3," Blue Letter Bible, https://www.blueletterbible.org/Comm/archives/guzik_david/Study Guide_Gen/Gen_3.cfm/.

CHAPTER FOUR: Lord, Still My Soul

1. Augustine, *Confessions*, trans. Henry Chadwick (Oxford: Oxford University Press, 2008), 3.

2. "An Ode to Silence: Why You Need It in Your Life," Cleveland Clinic Health Essentials, August 7, 2020, https://health.clevelandclinic.org/why-you-need-more-silence-in-your-life/.

3. "An Ode to Silence."

4. Max Lucado, *Help Is Here: Finding Fresh Strength and Purpose in the Power of the Holy Spirit* (Nashville: Thomas Nelson, 2022), 67.

5. Thomas Scott Caulley, "Abba," in *Lexham Bible Dictionary*, ed. John D. Barry et al. (Bellingham, WA: Lexham, 2016).

CHAPTER FIVE: Lord, Reveal Yourself to Me

1. A. W. Tozer, *The Knowledge of the Holy: The Attributes of God: Their Meaning in the Christian Life* (San Francisco: HarperOne, 2009), 56.

2. Tozer, *The Knowledge of the Holy*, 60.

3. Lysa TerKeurst and Joel Muddamalle, *Seeing Jesus in the Old Testament: He's Never Absent, We're Never Alone* (Matthews, NC: Proverbs 31 Ministries, 2021), 32.

4. R. C. Sproul, "The Holy Love of God," Ligonier, June 25, 2014, https://www.ligonier.org/learn/articles/holy-love-god/.

CHAPTER SIX: Lord, Teach Me to Pray

1. Max Lucado, *You Can Count on God: 365 Devotions* (Nashville: Thomas Nelson, 2021), 38.

2. C. H. Spurgeon, "Unanswered Prayer," Sermon No. 3344, March 6, 1913, https://www.spurgeongems.org/sermon/chs3344.pdf, p. 1.

3. Spurgeon, "Unanswered Prayer," 1–2 (emphasis original).

4. John Piper, "Ask Your Father in Heaven," Desiring God, December 31, 2006, https://www.desiringgod.org/messages/ask-your-father-in -heaven/. Emphasis original.

5. Jodie Berndt, *Praying the Scriptures for Your Adult Children: Trusting God with the Ones You Love* (Grand Rapids: Zondervan, 2017), 16–17.

Proverbs 31
MINISTRIES

Know the Truth. Live the Truth. It changes everything.

If you were inspired by this study and desire to deepen your own personal relationship with Jesus Christ, Proverbs 31 Ministries has just what you are looking for.

Proverbs 31 Ministries exists to be a trusted friend who will take you by the hand and walk by your side, leading you one step closer to the heart of God through:

- Free online daily devotions
- First 5 Bible study app
- Online Bible studies
- Podcast
- COMPEL writer training
- She Speaks Conference
- Books and resources

Our desire is to help you to know the Truth and live the Truth. Because when you do, it changes everything.

For more information about Proverbs 31 Ministries, visit: www.Proverbs31.org.

Printed in the USA
CPSIA information can be obtained
at www.ICGtesting.com
JSHW011145110923
47994JS00002B/3